CULTURE SMART!

GERMANY

Barry Tomalin

Graphic Arts Center Publishing®

DD
61
.T643
2003

First published in Great Britain 2003
by Kuperard, an imprint of Bravo Ltd.

Copyright © 2003 Kuperard

Series Editor Geoffrey Chesler
Design DW Design

Simultaneously published in the U.S.A. and Canada
by Graphic Arts Center Publishing Company
P. O. Box 10306, Portland, OR 97296-0306

Third printing 2006

Library of Congress Cataloging-in-Publication Data

Tomalin, Barry, 1942-
  Germany : a quick guide to customs and etiquette / Barry
Tomalin.
    p. cm. — (Culture smart!)
Includes bibliographical references and index.
ISBN 1-55868-704-1 (alk. paper)
1. Germany—Social life and customs. 2. Etiquette—Germany. 3.
National characteristics, German. I. Title. II. Series.
DD61.T64 2003
943—dc21

                              2002015786

Printed in Malaysia

Cover image: Baroque gable, Rothenburg, Bavaria.
Travel Ink/Andrew Cowin

CultureSmart!Consulting and **Culture Smart!** guides both contribute
to and regularly feature in the weekly travel program "Fast Track"
on BBC World TV.

About the Author

BARRY TOMALIN is an expert on the business culture of Germany, having worked as a consultant with five German companies in Munich, Berlin, and Hamburg. He is the lead consultant of **CultureSmart!**Consulting, and the author of many books on culture and on cultural training. He has a BA in anthropology and linguistics from the University of London, and is a module leader on the MA program in media, technology, and culture studies at the University of Westminster in London.

Other Books in the Series

- Culture Smart! Argentina
- Culture Smart! Australia
- Culture Smart! Belgium
- Culture Smart! Brazil
- Culture Smart! Britain
- Culture Smart! Czech Republic
- Culture Smart! Costa Rica
- Culture Smart! China
- Culture Smart! Denmark
- Culture Smart! Finland
- Culture Smart! France
- Culture Smart! Greece
- Culture Smart! Hong Kong
- Culture Smart! India
- Culture Smart! Ireland
- Culture Smart! Italy
- Culture Smart! Japan
- Culture Smart! Korea
- Culture Smart! Mexico
- Culture Smart! Netherlands
- Culture Smart! Czech Republic
- Culture Smart! Philippines
- Culture Smart! Poland
- Culture Smart! Portugal
- Culture Smart! Russia
- Culture Smart! Singapore
- Culture Smart! Spain
- Culture Smart! Sweden
- Culture Smart! Switzerland
- Culture Smart! Thailand
- Culture Smart! Turkey
- Culture Smart! Ukraine
- Culture Smart! USA
- Culture Smart! Vietnam

Other titles are in preparation. For more information, contact: info@kuperard.co.uk

The publishers would like to thank **CultureSmart!**Consulting for its help in researching and developing the concept for this series.

contents

contents

Map of Germany

introduction

The Culture Smart! guides are written for people who want more than just the nuts and bolts of where to stay, what to see, and how to travel. They deal with the richly rewarding human dimension of foreign travel by telling you about the beliefs and attitudes of the people you will meet and about situations you may encounter. They help you to understand what makes people tick, the values they live by, and the kind of behavior they will reciprocate with goodwill and hospitality.

Germany is a powerful country that in many respects, despite superficial appearances, operates very differently from the U.S.A. and Britain. Understanding the nature of the differences will help you to achieve good relationships with the people you meet.

An informed and sympathetic approach is particularly valuable if you are visiting Germany for more than a few days as a casual tourist and need to understand how the Germans live and work. With chapters on core values and social attitudes, and a detailed and practical business briefing, *Culture Smart! Germany* offers a valuable introduction to the German way of life. It tells you what treatment to expect, what pitfalls to avoid, and how to build rapport and credibility with the German people.

In recent years Germany has successfully reunited its two halves, split asunder by the Allied powers after the devastation of the Second World War. The reabsorption, after over fifty years of Communist rule, of what was the German Democratic Republic into the liberal, free-market Federal Republic of Germany is a tribute to German determination, prosperity, and organizational talent. Despite economic downturns and painful restructuring, Germany today is a major world economic and diplomatic player that needs to be understood.

The beauty of Germany and the hospitality of her people make her a magnet for visitors from all over the world. This volume sets out to show you how to be a good and sensitive guest. The German people have a strong sense of social responsibility, and the guidelines given in these pages will prepare you to fit in with the social rules and regulations they live by in order to ensure a secure and harmonious lifestyle.

Culture Smart! Germany will help you to get the very best out of your visit. It will open doors for you and, we hope, lead you toward a lasting relationship with this culturally rich and varied people at the heart of Europe.

Enjoy the journey!

Key Facts

Official Name	Bundesrepublik Deutschland	The German Federal Republic is a full member of the European Union and of NATO.
Capital City	Berlin	
Main Cities	Berlin, Hamburg, Munich, Cologne, Frankfurt/Main.	
Area	137,828 sq. miles (356,974 sq. km.)	
Climate	Temperate	
Currency	Euro	Germany has been a member of the Eurozone since January 1, 2002.
Population	82 million	The most populous country in modern Europe.
Ethnic Makeup	91.5 % German 8.5 % others	Other nationalities residing in Germany include Turks, former Yugoslav nationals, Italians, Greeks, and others.
Family Makeup	The average family size is 2.7 people. The average number of children per family is 1.7.	
Language	German	Sorbian (Balto/Slavic), Frisian and Danish minority languages are spoken in the north of Germany.

Religion	38% Protestant (Lutheran); 34% Roman Catholic; 1.7% Moslem; 26.3% others.	Everyone pays a *Kirchensteuer* or church tax of 4% of income.
Government	Germany is a federal republic of sixteen states (or *Länder*). The seat of Government is in the capital, Berlin. There is an elected Head of State and an elected Head of Government. There are two Houses of Parliament, the *Bundestag* and the *Bundesrat*. Germany is a democracy with six political parties in the *Bundestag*.	
Media	ARD is the national TV and radio network, comprising North German, Bavarian and South German State TV and radio. There are also numerous local stations and commercial satellite stations. Of the large numbers of regional and national newspapers and magazines, the *Frankfurter Allgemeine Zeitung* and *Der Spiegel* are two of the most respected.	
Media: English Language	*Frankfurter Allgemeine* has a website with local and international English-language news available.	
Electricity	220 Volts, 50 Hz.	Two-pronged plugs used. Adaptors needed for US appliances.
Video/TV	PAL B system	NTSC TV will not work here.
Telephone	Germany's country code is 49.	To dial out, dial 00. Private companies may have special codes.

LAND & PEOPLE

The 82.1 million people of the Federal Republic of Germany occupy a landmass of 356,974 square kilometers (137,828 square miles) at the very heart of Europe. Not the largest country in Europe but the powerhouse of the European Union, Germany is a beautiful, varied, and fascinating place to live, work, or visit. The impact of her scholars, scientists, artists, musicians, writers, philosophers, and politicians on European culture has been profound, and has influenced much of the way the modern world thinks and acts.

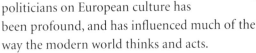

Although Germany had been settled for thousands of years, it became a single political entity only in 1871, when it was unified under Wilhelm I of Prussia by the statesman Otto von Bismarck. Who, then, are the German people, where did they come from, and what are they like today? A good way to start is by taking a look at the land that has shaped the people.

GEOGRAPHICAL SNAPSHOT

Germany occupies a pivotal position in Central Europe, bounded to the north by the North Sea, Denmark, and the Baltic Sea; to the east by Poland and the Czech Republic; to the south by Austria and Switzerland; and to the west by France, Luxembourg, Belgium, and the Netherlands. So many neighboring territories have always created a security problem and, with historically shifting borders, German-speaking populations have periodically found themselves incorporated into other countries. This is particularly true of the Alsace region of France and the German-speaking part of Switzerland. Until unification in 1871 the word "Germany" had been a geographical term, referring to an area occupied by small states, ruled by priests and princes, and for much of its history under the dominance of Rome and the Holy Roman Empire that succeeded it.

Germany has a wide variety of landscapes. There are three main geographical regions: the lowland plain in the north, the uplands in the center, and a mountainous region in the south. The lowlands include several river valleys and a large area of heathland (the Lüneburger Heide, the oldest national park in Germany).

At sea level on the North Sea and Baltic coasts there are sand dunes, marshlands, and several islands including the North Friesian islands, the

South Friesian islands, Rügen, and Heligoland in the North Sea. The eastern part of the lowland plain is Germany's breadbasket, rich in agricultural land. Between Hanover in the north and the River Main in the south are Germany's uplands with low mountains, valleys, and river basins. The mountains include the Taunus and Spessart ranges, and the Fichtelgebirge in the east.

The part of Germany best known to visitors is probably the southwestern mountain region containing the Black Forest (Schwarzwald), where the famous *Schwarzwälderkirschtorte* (a chocolate, cream, kirsch, and cherry cake) comes from. In the far south are the Bavarian Alps with Germany's highest peak, the Zugspitze, at 9,718 feet (2,962 meters).

The other major feature of the German landscape is its rivers. The most important of these is the Rhine, which rises in Switzerland and flows along the border with France before entering Germany proper and eventually flowing out through the Netherlands to the North Sea. The Rhine is both a major water transportation network and home to some of Germany's most beautiful scenery. Magnificent fortress-castles guard its banks. Vineyards cascade down the hill slopes to the river and its tributaries, the Mosel and the Neckar, yielding the grapes that produce the Hocks and Rieslings for which Germany is so well known. The Ruhr, traditional center of German industry, is also a tributary of the Rhine. The Elbe rises in the Czech Republic and flows northwest across the German plain to the North Sea, and the Danube (in German, Donau) rises on the eastern slopes of the Black Forest and flows eastward before entering Austria. The Oder and Neisse rivers form the international border with Poland in the east. Other major rivers are the Main, the Weser, and the Spree.

There are many large lakes on the northeastern plain, but those in the mountainous south are more dramatic. The most famous of these is Lake Constance (Bodensee).

Some 30 percent of the countryside is unspoilt woodland, but agriculture is now a minor part of the German economy, consisting mainly of small holdings run by individual farmers, many with other jobs. About 6 percent of the population are employed in farming.

So Germany, historically and today, is a focal point of European interaction, both through its nine bordering states and through its waterways carrying goods from all over Europe to the North Sea and Baltic ports.

CLIMATE

Germany's climate is temperate. The northern lowlands are slightly warmer than the mountainous south, which gets most of the rain and snow. The average rainfall is 23–27 inches (600–700 mm) a year. Temperatures range from 21°F (–6°C) in the mountains, and 35°F (1.5°C) in the lowlands, in winter, to 64°F (18°C), and even 68°F (20°C) in the valleys, in summer.

The *Föhn*

A peculiar feature of the Alpine climate in southern Germany is the *Föhn*. This is a warm, dry wind that blows down the leeward slope of a mountain. As moist air rises up the windward side, it cools and loses its moisture. When it descends it heats up because of the increase in pressure, and can cause a 10° rise in temperature in a short period. The Föhn brings clear, warm weather, and is often marked by beautiful twilight periods. Expect sudden atmospheric changes.

THE GERMAN PEOPLE: A BRIEF HISTORY

Every country has its own founding myth. In Britain it is the story of the Celts, King Arthur, and the mysterious land of Avalon. In the United States it is the story of the Founding Fathers.

"Germany" was not a name chosen by peoples who inhabited the area. "Germania" was the name they were given by the Roman historian Tacitus, who rather admired them.

The original Germans were hunter-gatherers who seem to have migrated westward and southward from Asia and from northeastern Europe around 2300 BCE, and who settled in the area of the River Danube. They seem to have arrived in two main waves. The first were Celtic peoples, who raised crops, bred livestock, and traded with their Mediterranean neighbors. Archeological finds suggest that these people were among the first to develop copper and tin mining, and to make implements and containers out of bronze. Later arrivals, probably originally from southern Russia, moved into north and central Germany, and these are the  real ancestors of the German-speaking peoples. They introduced the use of iron, developed metal tools and weapons, and eventually absorbed the peoples of the existing Celtic Bronze Age culture.

The German tribes spread along the north-eastern frontier of the Roman Empire and became Rome's most ferocious opponents. A founding myth of Germany is the famous victory over the

Roman legions by Hermann (Latin, Arminius), a chieftain of the Cherusci tribe, in a battle in the Teutoburg forest in 9 CE. The Teutoburge Wald remains sacred to German memory to this day.

The movie *Gladiator*, you may remember, begins with a battle fought by the Roman army under the Emperor Marcus Aurelius (161–180 CE) against the invading German hordes. As Roman power declined, so the German tribes advanced, eventually sacking Rome itself in 410 CE.

The Carolingian Empire

German history proper begins with the conquests of the Frankish king Karl der Grosse, better known as Charlemagne, who succeeded in a short period in consolidating the Germanic tribes, converting pagans, and imposing order on the whole of continental Europe. His capital at Aachen in North Rhine-Westphalia became the center of a renaissance of learning. He also promoted the Frankish tongue.

During the first millennium of the Christian Era borders in Europe were fluid, first determined by the needs of the Roman Empire, and later influenced by dynastic marriages and the Church. With the collapse of the Roman Empire in the West, the Church in Rome became the sole heir and transmitter of imperial culture and legitimacy. Charlemagne, as the champion of

Christendom, revived the title of "Roman emperor" and in 800 CE was crowned Holy Roman Emperor by Pope Leo III in Rome. The new line of "Roman" emperors he inaugurated lasted for more than a thousand years, although they seldom had any power outside the boundaries of Germany. After his death, the empire he had created began to fragment, partly owing to the peculiarly German laws of inheritance that apportioned land equally among sons. Nevertheless, a series of vigorous German kings tried to convert the Roman empire of the West into reality, which brought them into conflict with the Popes and the revived city-republics of Italy. This struggle became a major factor in the political history of the Middle Ages.

During the Middle Ages the German princes consolidated their landholdings, originally held as fiefs granted by the Holy Roman Emperor. Gradually these principalities became more independent, uniting only to elect one of their number as Holy Roman Emperor on the death of his predecessor. By the sixteenth century, the title had become hereditary, and had passed to a single German dynasty—the Austrian House of Habsburg. After the Thirty Years' War (1618–48) between Protestants and Catholics in Central Europe, the Holy Roman Emperor's authority in Germany was greatly reduced.

What we know today as Germany was thus a patchwork of small autonomous principalities, duchies, kingdoms, and a few free cities, owing a loose allegiance to the Holy Roman Emperor. This situation lasted until the Holy Roman Empire was dissolved by Napoleon in 1806.

Some German cities had acquired a special status. Foremost among these were the members of the Hanseatic League, a medieval confederation of north German cities with a monopoly on the North Sea and Baltic trade. The Hansa towns, which included Bremen, Hamburg, and Lübeck, traded overseas and had a leading commercial role in what was a largely agricultural economy.

The Reformation
In 1517, the Augustinian monk Martin Luther initiated the Protestant Reformation in Germany by protesting publicly against the Vatican's sale of indulgences (promises freeing the bearer from all his or her sins). His protests found an echo in many of the north German principalities and a number of them adopted the Protestant Lutheran

religion. Political, economic, and religious interests soon became intertwined. In the following century the Electors of the Holy Roman Empire were deeply divided into Catholic and Protestant camps. A revolt by the Bohemian (Czech) nobles against the proposed accession to the throne of Bohemia of the Habsburg Emperor's cousin, Ferdinand of Styria, soon triggered a wider conflict. Ferdinand became Holy Roman Emperor the following year, and the resultant Thirty Years' War engulfed Germany, Austria, Sweden, the Netherlands, and France. One legacy of the struggle between the Catholic and Protestant states is the split today between the mainly Protestant north Germany and the mainly Catholic south.

The Rise of Prussia

Crucial to understanding the development of modern Germany is the rise of Prussia. Officially abolished in 1947, in the postwar division of Germany, the Prussian state embodied much that seems quintessentially German—discipline, efficiency, militarism, and the dominance of the Junker aristocratic class. Interestingly, Prussia emerged relatively late in German history. Situated in the northeast of Germany, from the thirteenth to the sixteenth centuries it was an undeveloped wasteland, a little like the American West at the beginning of the nineteenth century, inhabited by pagan Prussian and Lithuanian tribes. It was formed and governed by the Teutonic Knights, a chivalric order of military monks, an offshoot of the Knights Templar, whose mission was to convert the Baltic peoples to Christianity. At their height they controlled an area the size of Great Britain from their capital at Marienburg, present-day Malbork in Poland.

The Teutonic Knights were heavily defeated by a Polish-Lithuanian army at the Battle of Tannenberg in 1410. In 1525 under the influence of Martin Luther, their Grand Master, Prince Albrecht of Hohenzollern, converted to Protestantism and the Order itself was secularized. The brethren began to marry and hold land, and soon became a new military aristocracy. In the same year Albrecht transformed Prussia into a hereditary duchy, owing suzerainty to Poland. In 1618 Prussia passed by inheritance to the Hohenzollern Electors of Brandenburg, who consolidated and expanded its power. Polish sovereignty was thrown off by Friedrich Wilhelm, the "Great Elector," and so was born a vigorous new power, whose noble or "Junker" class was steeped in a long martial tradition.

Prussia became a kingdom in 1701, and rose to international prominence in the eighteenth century under Friedrich II, known as "the Great," who built an army of such efficiency and might that its soldiers were crucial in maintaining the European balance of power. For example, at the Battle of Waterloo against Napoleon, in 1815, it was General Blücher's Prussian troops who turned the tide of battle in the Allies' favor. Nationalist reaction to the creation of the Napoleonic Empire was a spur to internal social and administrative reform and Prussian regeneration.

Following the defeat of Napoleon, the victorious Allies created a new German Confederation to fill the void left by the destruction of the Holy Roman Empire. This association of states was dominated by Austria until after 1848. By the middle of the nineteenth century, however, Prussia had emerged as the most powerful German state and a deadly rival of Austria. Prussia's aim, the plan of its Chancellor,

Prince Otto von Bismarck, was to unite the German nation under its leadership. Austria's policy was to control a divided Germany. The determining factor was the strength and organization of the Prussian army, and the decisive battle took place in 1866.

Prussia's other main rival in Europe was France, and in 1870 Bismarck succeeded in maneuvering the French Emperor Napoleon III into declaring war. After inflicting a humiliating defeat on the French in 1870, in 1871 Bismarck declared Kaiser Wilhelm I Emperor of a united Germany, with its capital at Berlin, in an historic ceremony in the hall of mirrors of the palace at Versailles.

The new German Empire thus came into being with little experience of democracy, but great experience of military organization and campaigning. The huge organizing power and energy of Germany was soon evident in the speed of its industrialization—by 1900 German industrial output matched the achievements of first Britain and then America in the century and a half before. Bismarck, the architect of German unification, became the first Chancellor of the Empire, but was later dropped by the Kaiser's successor, Wilhelm II. It was Wilhelm II who precipitated the First World War (1914–18), which not only engulfed Europe but saw American troops fighting in Europe for the first time.

The Weimar Republic

Anger with Germany for causing the First World War led the victorious Allies to impose crippling reparation payments, while cutting Germany back to its pre-1914 borders. In 1919 a National Constituent Assembly met at Weimar, on the River Elbe, to draw up a new, democratic constitution. One could argue that the young Weimar Republic never stood much of a chance, sandwiched as it was between the demands of an aggressive Communist party (fired by the recent success of the Russian Revolution of 1917) on the left, and the rise of National Socialism (fueled by resentment of the unfair burden of reparations, the loss of German territory, and the social dislocation brought about the by the Great Depression of the early 1930s) on the right.

The National Socialist, or Nazi, party won the elections of 1932 with 37.3 percent of the vote, and by 1933 its leader Adolf Hitler was both Chancellor and Head of State of the Third German Reich.

The Third Reich

Hitler aggressively pursued his aim of making Germany great again by building up the German army, navy, and airforce, and seeking to reverse the territorial losses of World War One. Annexation of the Rhineland was followed by the invasion of Austria, the Sudetenland, and then the rest of Czechoslovakia. Ruthlessly crushing all internal opposition, he created a totalitarian dictatorship that indoctrinated the public with Nazi ideology, and set out to realize its dream of creating a racially pure Aryan nation by forcibly acting against "undesirable" groups—not only dissidents, but also Romanies, Russians, prostitutes, homosexuals, and, above all, Jews. In 1939, flush with his earlier successes, he plunged Germany once more into war by invading Poland.

During the Second World War the Nazis engaged in slave labor, plunder, and mass extermination, building concentration camps throughout central and eastern Europe for this purpose. In the Holocaust between 1939 and 1945 an estimated six million European Jews died in the camps, as well as millions of others besides.

Post-War Germany

In 1945, after six years of total war, Germany was utterly defeated, and economically and politically destroyed. It was occupied by the four main Allied powers—the U.S.A., the U.K., France, and the Soviet Union—and its capital Berlin came under four-power control. In 1948 differences between Russia and the Western powers led to the complete breakdown of the joint Allied machinery for the control of Germany, and the Soviet Union imposed a blockade on Berlin, cutting off all land routes from the West. In what is known as the Berlin Airlift, from June 1948 to September 1949 the Americans and British ferried two and a quarter million tons of supplies into the beleaguered city by air along a twenty-three-mile-wide air corridor until the Soviets were obliged to back down.

In 1949 the country was partioned into the Western, democratic, Federal Republic of Germany, with its capital in the university city of Bonn, and the Communist German Democratic Republic, with its capital in East Berlin. Berlin itself remained divided into zones controlled by the occupying powers, and was linked to West Germany by an air and road corridor. It continued to be a flashpoint in the "Cold War" between the West and the Soviet Union, and was the subject of many spy stories by novelists such as John le Carré and Len Deighton. An uprising in East Berlin was suppressed by Soviet troops in 1953. In 1955 West Germany became a member of NATO, and East Germany joined the Warsaw Pact. In 1961 the Communist regime built the Berlin Wall to stop its citizens from emigrating to West Berlin. Escapees were shot on sight.

The Economic Miracle

The main incentives for the would-be emigrants were the climate of freedom and the immensely higher standard of living in West Germany. The socialist republic of East Germany was economically stagnant. America's farsighted postwar Marshall Plan for aid to West Germany had enabled it to recreate its industrial base. Such was its success that under the first postwar Chancellor, Dr. Konrad Adenauer, West German output rapidly overtook that of every other country in Europe. In 1956 West Germany became one of the founding members of the European Economic Union.

German Reunification

The East German state—modeled on and dominated by the Soviet Union—controlled the lives of its citizens with an iron grip. Encouraged by the relaxation of the Soviet Communist regime by General Secretary Mikhail Gorbachev, in the 1980s East Germans began to seek new escape routes to the West through Hungary and Austria. The leak became a flood when, on November 9, 1989, the Berlin Wall was breached dramatically, and subsequently dismantled. With the bloodless collapse of the East German regime, West and East Germany were reunited in the German Federal Republic in October 1990, and the capital was moved from Bonn to Berlin.

THE GERMAN PEOPLE TODAY

Today Germany is struggling to integrate its two communities, and to regenerate the East and bring it up to the economic standards of the West. Berlin has once again become the capital of a united nation and the five neue Länder (new states), as the East German states are known, are becoming progressively part of the overall German order. It has been a difficult and heroic task that has brought huge economic and social problems. The citizens of East Germany were for years cut off from the changes taking place in Western Europe, and there can be considerable tension between the "Ossies" (Easterners) who often feel disadvantaged to the benefit of their "Wessie" (Western) cousins. The five "Ossie" states are Mecklenburg, Brandenburg, Saxony, Saxony-Anhalt, and Thuringia.

Germany is a remarkably cohesive ethnic community in which 99 percent of the population are native German. However, the Turkish *Gastarbeiter*, or "guest workers," are a growing minority. Germany is increasingly home to refugees from Central Europe and from the Balkans. Your taxi driver is just as likely to be Iranian, or Kosovan, as German.

The east-west division will fade away as economic standards and lifestyles even out, but the north-south contrast will remain. Broadly speaking, Germany divides into Prussia in the north and the southern states. There is no clear dividing line but round about Frankfurt the southern Länder begin. There are minor distinctions in accent and vocabulary, but the key distinctions are in religion and lifestyle. The "Prussian" north is Protestant, hard-working, highly structured, and formal; the south is largely Catholic, and is relatively more relaxed and easygoing.

Because Germany is essentially regional, with each state having its own government and legislature and sending delegates to the Bundestag (parliament) in Berlin, there is no major rivalry between north and south, such as you might find in the U.S.A. or Britain, but you will notice definite differences in lifestyle, and a German may identify himself or herself as a native of a particular area, rather than as simply German.

GERMANY'S CITIES

Until 1989, Bonn, a university city near Cologne, was the capital of West Germany, and the eastern sector of Berlin the East German capital. After reunification the Federal Government began a staged move back to Berlin, a process completed in 2003. Apart from Berlin, the capital, and Hamburg, its major seaport, Germany's major cities are mainly in the uplands and the south. Munich (München) is an important commercial and cultural center, Cologne (Köln) an industrial city with a famous cathedral, and Heidelberg a major university city. Essen is Germany's steel capital on the River Ruhr, Dortmund its coal mining center, and Stuttgart in the south an important commercial and industrial center— and home of Daimler Benz. (Volkswagen is based in Wolfsburg, BMW in Munich.) Düsseldorf is a center of fashion and commerce. Leipzig, one of the oldest university towns and a major trade center, cut off for years in East Germany, is now regaining its prominence. And Frankfurt-am-Main is one of the world's great financial centers.

One of the characteristics of German cities is that they are often surrounded by forest. Flying into even such a large city as Frankfurt you are impressed by the number of pine trees and fields around it. Germany is one of the most ecologically minded countries in Europe, if not the world. The combination of strong regional character, limited local populations, and green surroundings gives Germany a sense of being uncrowded.

GERMAN GOVERNMENT

Germany is a federation divided into sixteen *Länder* (states) of considerable autonomy. The governing constitution of the country, established in 1949 and since 1990 modified to include the East German states, is the *Grundgesetzt*, or Basic Law. This provides a federal constitution with a President as Head of State, elected for a five-year term by both houses of the Bundestag.

The Bundestag, or Parliament, constitutionally contains two houses with 656 members. In the lower house, the Bundestag, members are elected for a four-year term. The upper house, the Bundesrat, is made up of representatives from the *Land* parliaments. Each state has up to six seats depending on its population.

The President is responsible for appointing the chief minister, or Chancellor, whose appointment must be ratified by both houses of the Bundestag. He holds office for four years. The Chancellor appoints his ministers, who are also ratified by Parliament.

State	Capital	Characteristic
Schleswig-Holstein	Kiel	North
Mecklenburg-West Pomerania (Mecklenburg-Vorpommern)	Schwerin	North
Hamburg	Hamburg	One of the three "city states" North
Bremen	Bremen	One of the three "city states" North
North Rhine-Westphalia (Nordrhein-Westfalen)	Düsseldorf	North
Lower Saxony (Niedersachsen)	Hanover (Hannover)	North
Berlin	Berlin	One of the three "city states" North
Brandenburg	Potsdam	North
Saxony (Sachsen)	Dresden	North
Rhineland Palatinate (Rheinland-Pfalz)	Mainz	South
Saarland	Saarbrücken	South
Hesse (Hessen)	Wiesbaden	South
Saxony-Anhalt (Sachsen-Anhalt)	Magdeburg	North
Thuringia (Thüringen)	Erfurt	South
Baden-Württemberg	Stuttgart	South
Bavaria (Bayern)	Munich (München)	South

Germany is a multiparty democracy. If you can win 5 percent of the vote in an election then you are entitled to a seat in the Bundestag. The main political parties are shown below.

CDU – Christian Democratic Party
Center-right, founded by Dr. Konrad Adenauer after the Second World War. Traditionally the party of business and agriculture, it is probably closest in spirit to the Republican Party in the U.S.A .and the Conservative Party in the U.K.

SPD – Social Democratic Party
Center-left, the oldest party in Germany, with its roots in working-class politics. Now the party of the professional classes and white-collar workers. Its first leader to become Chancellor was the former mayor of Berlin, Willy Brandt. It is the party of Liberal values and is probably closest to the Democratic Party in the U.S.A. and the Labour Party in the U.K.

CSU – Christian Social Union
Center-right, generally considered the Bavarian equivalent of the CDU, with which it is allied.

FDP – Free Democratic Party
Centrist, a smaller party with politically progressive but economically conservative values. It forms coalitions with the CDU or SPD.

PDS – Party of Democratic Socialism
This is the former Communist Party that ruled East Germany before it was reintegrated into the German Federal Republic in 1990. Its membership tends to be largely East German, and its main function is to represent the interests of East Germans in the Bundestag. It is the smallest of the parties in the Bundestag.

The Greens/Alliance 90
The Greens and Alliance 90 are the ecological and antinuclear party of Germany and, as Greens, won their first seat in the Bundestag in 1983. The Green Party holds its seats in the Bundestag by virtue of its coalition with the Alliance 90 Party. This is a civil rights party that campaigned for the reunification of Germany.

AMERICAN INFLUENCE

The political and cultural impact of the United States on modern Germany has been profound. Because of its frontline status in the Cold War, American troops only finally left German soil in 1993. A little-recognized but formative influence was ASFN, the American Forces Network radio station that broadcast US pop music and news for American personnel and Germans alike. Two generations of West Germans were brought up on American pop and rock classics.

THE EUROZONE

As a member of the European Union and of the Eurozone (Germany has replaced the Deutschmark with the Euro), the German government is also responsible for upholding European laws, as well as enacting its own.

Germany today is a leading industrial European power, firmly committed to democracy and a major influence in the development of post-Communist central and southern Europe. German investment in the former countries of the USSR and in the Balkans is greater than that of any other European country except Russia. Above all, Germany is deeply committed to the development of a united Europe, politically as well as economically, devoting its immense energy and resources to that end.

VALUES & ATTITUDES

The shared values and attitudes of a nation determine its political, economic, and social structures and the behavior of its citizens. What the Germans as a people prioritize as core values will often differ from what, say, Americans and British people would prioritize, even if a considerable number of them originate from the same common stock. Where then, to put it simply, are the Germans "coming from"? What makes them tick, both in business and socially?

Among the first things anybody who hears the word "German" thinks of are efficiency and organization. These are not terms one would normally associate with national character, so where does this perception come from? Anywhere you go in Germany you will meet a high degree of tidiness and organization, applied down to the last detail. The Germans themselves, however, don't think in these terms. They think in terms of order. Efficiency and organization are by-products of the search for order. Order is a fundamental German value, and it permeates everything they do.

ORDNUNG MUSS SEIN

A key concept in German life, therefore, is *Ordnung,* or order. The phrase "*Ordnung muss sein*" means that order "must be." It reflects the belief that there is an inherent order and system in everything. The object of life is to analyze everything to find that order and system, and then to apply it. Inculcating that search for order and meaning, and showing how it is applied, is the function of German education and social training. Order is what gives a secure basis to life. Disorder is deeply unsettling for the Germans, and therefore their first aim in any difficult situation is to search for and reestablish order.

"So what?" you may respond. "Everybody likes a tidy life." Indeed so, but in German thinking order is raised to a national idea, and it has ramifications in every aspect of national life.

An example of this is planning. A German firm will plan an event months ahead, knowing that circumstances are likely to change before the event itself. Their search for order means that they prefer to spend time replanning every time circumstances change rather than to leave the whole thing until a short time before (as the French, Italians, and Spaniards might do) and just do it once.

We all have a number of characteristics drummed into us by upbringing, education, and experience that we carry around with us as part of our individual psychological and social programing. One of these may be a need for order in our life. But this remains an individual preoccupation, not a social one. Imagine order as a national internal principle. Imagine a situation in which it is more difficult not to pick up litter and put it in a waste bin than it is to leave it on the ground. There you have the German psyche—a national sense of internalized social order. This has all sorts of effects on people's behavior. For example, it helps to explain why the Germans are the most ecologically minded people in Europe, and why they will readily rebuke strangers for minor transgressions, such as jaywalking, or antisocial acts that other people might silently suffer or simply ignore.

A national mindset that puts order first has a number of consequences. Firstly, if you elect a leader, you will tend to want to do what he or she says, so respect for authority is important. Secondly, it means that you will approve of people who plan ahead, organize, and check, and disapprove of people who tend to improvise or do things "on the fly." If you are by nature a "last minuter," or, in British terms, "a muddle througher," you will need to brush up your performance if you are dealing with the German sense of order.

All this has contributed to the widely held stereotype of a humorless nation that rigidly organizes itself and follows orders without question. This is simply not true. The Germans have as great a sense of humor as anyone and can be deeply and explosively rebellious, as the amazing and world-changing breaching of the Berlin Wall in 1989 showed. There are also differences in the way north and south Germany interpret the notion of order as a social principle. Nevertheless, it is important to recognize that this organizing principle of German society is deeply rooted and must be taken into account.

KLARHEIT

An English and German manager sat down to discuss a project. After a long, analytical examination of all the ins and outs the German manager finally came up with a scheme he was happy with. "Good," he said, "I have a clear system I feel comfortable with." The significant word is "clear." For most Germans it is important to be clear, and part of that clarity (*Klarheit*) is to have a system that outlines for everyone exactly what has to be done and who will do it. Isn't this the aim of all business, you may ask? Yes, but elevated to a national principle? No. It is very important for Germans to be direct and straightforward, and to avoid ambiguity both in their feelings and their communications. "*Alles klar,*" is a common way of acknowledging instructions and explanations.

To reach that clarity is not always an easy process and Germans will involve themselves (some say indulge themselves) in long, deep, and soul-searching analyses of situations or proposals to find the clarity from which that system will emerge. Once it has emerged, the system takes on the status of a pillar of order and is not easily changed. This accounts for what people see as a certain rigidity in the German way of doing things, and a certain lack of flexibility. Also, perhaps, an over-involvement in the minutiae of categorization. One of the problems of German business can be "analysis paralysis," where the process of analyzing a situation defeats the more important goal of reaching a decision.

Go to a bus stop. The bus arrives and at the last moment you realize that you can't buy your ticket on the bus. You ask the driver/conductor to let you on. The answer may well be "No." If you don't know the system, you can't use the service. If you want to find out, ask someone to tell you. It's all perfectly clear. You end up late at your destination and angry at the rigidity and lack of tolerance of the Germans. The bus driver thinks you are an uneducated, rude, and disorganized foreigner. After all, he or she is only observing the system.

On the other hand, individual Germans show an amazing amount of tolerance and courtesy to foreigners. They will go out of the way to educate you in or explain to you the system—sometimes to the foreigner's intense annoyance. "Who are these people to tell me what to do?" The answer is, "They're Germans. They've learned the system. They adhere to it. They see no reason why you shouldn't do so too. And they're prepared to take the responsibility for showing you. After all, isn't an organized life easier for everyone?"

TRUTH AND DUTY

To find a system that is clear and that works takes a lot of thinking and a degree of honesty. On the whole, Germans prefer to say what they think and to deal in what they see to be the truth. Frankness and straightforwardness to the point of bluntness are features of German society, emphasized even more strongly in the north than in the south. In negotiation, German business partners will have a much smaller gap between their entry and exit positions than their British or American counterparts. Germans and Americans both find the noncommittal nature and indirectness of much of British communication abhorrent. It is important in Germany to say what you mean. Fear of offending your partner is not a key consideration. This means that, however friendly and supportive they may be intended, German comments on behavior or character can often be uncomfortably direct. This isn't helped by the German use of English. Native English speech is full of "please," "thank you," "would," "could," and "might." Germans speaking English will use "yes," "no," "should," and "must," and so come across as uncompromising or just plain rude.

With this concern for truth and accuracy sometimes goes a certain literal-mindedness. In a language class in 1970s London, Helmut arrived late with a black eye, saying that he had been attacked on the tube (the underground rail system). The lesson stopped as his classmates asked him to explain. He had bought a joke phrase book, popular at the time, called *The Insults Dictionary: How to Insult People in Twenty Languages*, and had been trying it out. At first people had smiled or ignored him, but when he walked up to someone and said, "Move over, stupid!" the man had immediately hit him!

DUTY (*PFLICHTBEWUSSTSEIN*)

On a more serious note, what goes with this wish for honesty and clarity is a strong sense of duty. The other side of the phrase "Say what you

In a teamwork simulation between Irish, English, and German members of a financial services company the team make-up included two observers, one for each team. At the debrief stage the Irish member reported back, full of good humor and amusing asides, pointing out some of the flaws in her team's presentation. Then it was Heinz's turn. Heinz was an exceptionally good-looking, kind, and charming man from Munich whose English was excellent. He began like this. "I have ten points to make from my observation and they are these. First you didn't …. , secondly you should have done …. and you didn't. Thirdly you didn't . . . ." And so he went on.

At the break the British and Irish members got the facilitator in a corner. "Heinz really got our backs up," they said. "We could feel our shoulders rising with tension." The English facilitator had to agree. He had felt the same way, even though he had realized that Heinz was just following the German style of taking the good things for granted and explaining as clearly, straightforwardly, and concisely as he could what was wrong and the lessons to be learned. It was, if you like, a formidable feat of organization and synthesis, but a failure of diplomacy and rapport. Needless to say, Heinz's natural charm and courtesy in the break soon won everybody back over.

mean," is "Mean what you say." For someone to say something and not do it, or at least attempt to do it and explain the problems in good time, is seen very badly. If a German says, "I'll do my best" it means, "I will use my best efforts and probably succeed." If an English-speaker says it, on the other hand, it may well be an excuse for likely failure. Doing your duty is a very important part of German life, and applies as much to the person walking their dog and picking up and disposing of dog mess as it does in a military or business context.

This sense of duty is linked to a deeper tradition in German thought—a certain high-mindedness and a belief in higher principles that is reflected in the operas of Wagner or in the great Romantic poets Goethe and Schiller. Implicit in German intellectual life is a sense of the greater good. It is important to subordinate one's own will to the demands of the greater good. For the Germans the sense of *Gemeinschaft* (community) and *Gruppenzugehörigkeit* (group belonging) means that one does not act against the interests of the group, for one's own sake as much as for the good of others. The proverb "Do as you would be done by" sums up this sentiment very well. This form of idealism helps to explain why the Germans seem to have an internalized sense of public order.

An example of this shared sense of order is the Hauswoche (house week), typical of Baden-Würtenburg. The residents of an apartment block commonly set a rotation of responsibility for sweeping the street outside, washing the public corridors of the building, etc. This is clearly a limit on personal freedom, but they are happy to do it as they see it as contributing to the public good, their own included.

THE WORK ETHIC

To live life like this can take a fair amount of effort and it is no surprise that the Germans have a strong work ethic. Doing what needs to be done in the right way is an important part of the German psyche, and this extends as much to tidying up and organizing your personal space as it does to how you work.

Another aspect of the work ethic is thoroughness, or *Gründlichkeit*. If a job's worth doing, it's worth doing perfectly. A German employee transferred to a British company was impressed by the high targets he was set. No matter how hard he worked he never seemed able to hit his targets 100 percent. Concerned about this he approached his manager. "You're doing really well," he was amazed to be told. "Nobody expects you to hit more than 60 percent!"

The German work ethic is reinforced by the ideas of the Protestant Reformation, initiated by Luther in the sixteenth century and shared by northern European countries and by the United States, Canada, Australia, and New Zealand. According to this way of thinking, work is good in itself, and one's attitude to it and the disciplined way one goes about it is character-forming and purifying. Lutheranism, the religion of much of Germany, stresses the importance of hard work and prudent living as a way of personal development. The maintenance of a stable social order and a modest and prudent lifestyle are traditionally seen as part of the good religious life. (Something similar can also be found in countries such as Japan and Korea, deeply influenced by the Confucian ideals of hard work and modesty.) These attitudes are particularly strong in the Protestant north of Germany, influenced both by the Reformation and by the disciplined, militaristic tradition of Prussia.

Interestingly enough, you should not confuse the amount of work you do and how you organize it with the amount of time you spend doing it. Many people think that the Germans, like the Americans and increasingly the British, work every hour that God gives. In fact they don't. For them overtime, staying late, and taking work home are signs of personal inefficiency or a poor job description (organizational inefficiency), and are reasons for lack of confidence in a partner rather than confidence. For a German, the work ethic means that during your paid working hours you work as hard and in as disciplined and non-time-wasting a fashion as you can, but you don't stay late. It also means reliability. You will be there when you say you will be, you will stop when you say you will, and you will do what you have said you will do. No more, but certainly no less.

AUTHORITY AND STATUS

What holds the system in place is a strong sense of authority and status. The Germans, like anyone else, will criticize authority, but ultimately will accept it—in the home, the town council, the office, and the government. Adherence to reporting structures and systems is important. With it goes a strong sense of status. Good clothes, good food, good housing, and above all good cars are indications of status. For example, a human resources executive was organizing a conference in a small town. The occasion was the meeting of teams in a merger between two German companies, and the respective CEOs were intending to be present. In the conference hotel one CEO was offered the penthouse and the other CEO was offered the executive suite. But no, rather

A British manufacturer had won a contract to supply parts to a company in the north of Germany. To celebrate the deal he took the German team out to a Weinstube *(wine bar). The affair got very jolly, with the British manufacturer buying drinks all round and calling everyone* du *in a friendly, backslapping way. On his return home, he was astonished to receive a fax saying that the German company had decided not to go ahead with the deal. Aghast at the news he telephoned his German colleague to find out what had happened, and was told the German chairman had found it impossible to do business with him on account of his unacceptable behavior.*

Nothing the British businessman had done would have been in any way out of the ordinary at home, but in German terms he had overstepped the boundary between office courtesy and private life. For the British manufacturer it was a way of making friends with his new colleagues; for the German company chairman it threatened his respect and credibility and he could not let the relationship go any farther. This admittedly rather extreme example nevertheless illustrates the importance of keeping Dienst *and* Schnapps *firmly in their place.*

than accept the suite the other CEO preferred accommodation in a different hotel. In German business, particularly, parity of status is important.

PRIVATE AND PUBLIC

The Germans also make a strong distinction between work and play. "*Dienst ist Dienst und Schnapps ist Schnapps*," they say. "Work is work and drink is drink." Never the twain shall meet! Boundaries are important in German life, and there is a clear boundary between working time and play time. This compartmentalization is reflected in social life as well.

One possible reason the Germans are so insistent on keeping the barriers up and in place might be their own insecurity. Situated in the middle of Europe, bordered by nine countries, and with an often turbulent political and economic history, the Germans have been able to create their own internal sense of security. Perhaps in the European Union, with time, those barriers will come down.

chapter three

CUSTOMS &
TRADITIONS

Never assume that people who like to live an organized life don't know how to enjoy themselves. With a mixture of Catholic and Protestant traditions, the Germans have a wide variety of festivals, customs, and celebrations, some of them pretty lively. It's also worth remembering that many popular Christmas traditions—Christmas trees, decorations, and cards—were actually introduced to Britain by Queen Victoria's German consort, Prince Albert.

NATIONAL AND RELIGIOUS FESTIVALS

The key national festivals in Germany vary according to the state. There are eleven legal holidays in all of Germany, and some others that are celebrated in only a few (mainly Catholic) states, indicated by an asterisk* opposite.

Christmas

The main annual celebration is Christmas. For weeks before December 25, the date that

DATE	GERMAN FESTIVAL	ENGLISH NAME
January 1	*Neujahrstag*	New Year's Day
*January 6	*Heilige Drei Könige*	Epiphany (only in Baden-Württemberg, Bavaria, and Saxony-Anhalt)
March/April	*Karfreitag*	Good Friday
March/April	*Ostersonntag*	Easter Sunday
March/April	*Ostermontag*	Easter Monday
May 1	*Tag der Arbeit*	Labor Day/May Day
May/June	*Christi Himmelfahrtstag*	Ascension Day
May/June	*Pfingstsonntag*	Pentecost
May/June	*Pfingstmontag*	Monday after Pentecost
*May/June	*Fronleichnam*	Corpus Christi (only in Baden-Württemberg, Bavaria, Hesse, North Rhine-Westphalia, Rhineland Palatinate, and Saarland)
*August 15	*Mariä Himmelfahrt*	Assumption Day
October 3	*Tag der Deutschen Einheit*	Day of German Unity
*October 31	*Reformationstag*	Reformation Day (Protestant areas only)
*November 1	*Allerheiligen*	All Saints' Day (Catholic areas only)
November 21	*Busz- und Bettag*	Prayer and Atonement Day (now in Saxony only)
December 24	*Weihnachtsabend*	Christmas Eve
December 25	*Erster Weihnachtstag*	Christmas Day
December 26	*Zweiter Weihnachtstag*	Boxing Day

commemorates the birth of Christ, there are Christmas markets in town centers selling festive decorations, food, and wine. These have become popular with the coach-tour market, and coach parties from Britain, France, Belgium, and Italy now converge on German towns to enjoy the pre-Christmas festivities. One of the most famous of these is the *Christkindlemarkt* in Nuremberg (Nürnberg). At the Christmas market you can buy mulled wine (*Glühwein*), gingerbread (*Lebkuchen*), and also spicy Christmas cakes called *Stollen.* Choirs and brass bands sing and play Christmas carols.

A month before Christmas, the children start to open their *Adventskalender* (Advent calendar). The season of Advent, the four weeks leading up to Christmas, is a time of spiritual preparation for the faithful, and the Advent calendar contains a series of pictures illustrating Christmas themes, each concealed behind a scored paper door. The children open a new door every day to see what lies behind it during the run-up to Christmas.

Making one's own Christmas decorations is still popular in parts of Germany. In school, kindergarten, and even at home, children, teachers, and parents make decorations for the room and the Christmas tree. Another tradition observes Advent with a special wreath with four red candles called an *Adventskranz* (Advent wreath), one to be lit on each Sunday before Christmas.

On December 5 children leave out their (clean!) shoes when they go to bed (in some regions also socks). During the night St. Nikolaus (Father Christmas, or Santa Claus), is supposed to visit. If you've been good he leaves sweets, and if you've been bad he leaves twigs. On December 6 in many areas a man dressed up as St. Nikolaus visits schools and kindergartens. Children sing songs and, if they have been good throughout the year, are rewarded with sweets, nuts, oranges, and apples. He is followed by St. Nick's little helper, with a birch rod and a sack to carry away the naughty ones!

In Germany the Christmas family celebration takes place on Christmas Eve, December 24. Shops and offices close at midday, the family shares a light meal, and presents are exchanged round the Christmas tree. Who brings the presents? In north Germany it is *Weihnachtsmann* (a Father Christmas-like figure) and in south Germany it is the *Christkind* (represented as an angel). Traditionally families attend midnight mass on Christmas Eve.

By contrast, Christmas Day is a going-out day—families visit each other and youngsters play sports or go skiing. It is the equivalent of the British Boxing Day. By the way, the traditional German Christmas fare is goose with potatoes or dumplings and red cabbage rather than turkey.

New Year's Eve
December 31 is New Year's Eve, and New Year's Day on January 1 is a public holiday. It's a noisy affair with champagne and fireworks everywhere. Bells are rung in the churches to usher in the New Year, and in some places hot lead is dropped into water and the resulting strange shapes used to tell fortunes. Good luck charms may be exchanged, containing marzipan or chocolate images of horseshoes, ladybirds, four-leafed clovers, or even chimney sweeps and little pigs.

Epiphany
On January 6, the feast of the Epiphany celebrates the visit of the three kings to the stable where Christ was born. Called in German *Heilige Drei Könige* (Holy Three Kings), it is the occasion for children and teenage boys to dress up as the three wise men and go from door to door collecting money for charity. They generally get sweets or

candies as their reward. By the way, you may notice inside some doorways the chalked letters CMB. These initials, which stand for the Latin expression "Christ bless this house," show that a donation has been made to Sternsinger-Aktion. This is Germany's most successful charity. Every year youngsters from local churches raise several million euros for children in poor countries.

Karneval

Ash Wednesday, in Catholic parts of the country, signals the beginning of Lent, the period of fasting and purification leading up to Easter Sunday. The Sunday and Monday before Ash Wednesday is the time for *Karneval* (Carnival) in many towns and villages. Preparations for this start months before. The season begins on the eleventh day of the eleventh month at eleven minutes past eleven o'clock in the morning (on St. Martin's Day).

Karneval is a time of conviviality and informality, when the normally formal *Sie* (you) becomes the informal *du* for a short while. There are parties in offices, schools, and at home. People dress up in wild fancy-dress costumes and in the large cities there are big street processions.

Festivities reach their climax on *Rosenmontag* (Rose Monday), two days before Ash Wednesday. This is the day of the main *Karneval* parade, presided over by the *Karneval* "prince" and "princess." On *Fastnacht* (fast night), the final day of *Karneval* on Tuesday, there is no fasting but celebration and eating and drinking—the equivalent of Shrove Tuesday or Mardi Gras in the United States and Britain. *Weiberfastnacht* (women's fasting night) is on the Thursday before *Rosenmontag*. On this day women rule the city and have the right to cut in half the tie of any man they see. They actually do this, so if you are in Germany at this time be sure to wear an old tie!

In Munich *Karneval* is called *Fasching*. It is also known as *Fastnacht*, *Fasnet*, and *Fosnat*. The biggest and best celebrations take place in Düsseldorf, Mainz, and especially in Cologne.

Easter

Easter has its own traditions. The *Osterhase* (Easter rabbit) hides painted hard-boiled eggs for the children to hunt. The Sorbs (south of Berlin) are famous for their beautifully decorated Easter eggs. People exchange chocolate Easter eggs or chocolate rabbits. Those who have gardens bring in bare branches and decorate them with Easter flowers and other decorations. The Easter rabbit is a relic from the old pagan festival of the spring solstice, held to celebrate the renewal of the fertility of the land with the coming of spring after the sterility of winter.

The Easter church service itself follows the Crucifixion and miraculous Resurrection of Jesus Christ. On Good Friday, the church is empty; the statues of the saints are covered in black, and only the twelve Stations of the Cross—paintings, reliefs, or statues around the walls of the church depicting Christ's suffering and death on the cross—are left uncovered. A ceremony of prayer in front of each Station is observed. There are no flowers and no decorations. On Saturday the churches are closed except for private prayer, remembering the time Christ spent in the tomb. Then, on Easter Sunday morning, the covers are off, and the churches are filled with candles and flowers for the mass to celebrate Christ's Resurrection.

Germany's Baroque churches, all gleaming white and opulent color inside, are beautiful places to visit at any time, but they have a special excitement and radiance on Easter Sunday.

Other Religious Festivals
This pattern of decoration and celebration occurs with many saints' days, especially in rural areas. On St. Martin's Day in November, children carry paper lanterns through the streets. On Corpus Christi Day (the fortieth day after Easter), in Catholic areas, processions are held and outside altars erected and decorated.

Nonreligious Festivals

The tradition of decoration extends to
nonreligious occasions. For example, in the
Richtfest, or topping-out ceremony, when the shell
of a new building has been completed, flowers,
ribbons, and greenery are attached to the beams
before the roof is put on. Traditionally, a barrel of
beer is tapped and other refreshments are offered
by the owner.

On the first day of primary school parents give
their children a *Schultüte*. This is a cardboard
cone full of sweets, candies, pens, toys, and books
that is intended to sweeten the child's entry into
school. Sometimes these are almost as big as the
children themselves.

Oktoberfest

The *Oktober* festival
centered in Munich is
really a beer and wine
harvest festival. It lasts
for sixteen days, from late
September until the first Sunday in
October, and is the largest folk festival in Europe.
It started with the marriage of King Ludwig of
Bavaria to Princess Theresa of Saxe-
Hilburghausen. During the wedding celebration
people drank beer and wine in enormous tents
erected in the Theresienwiese field. This is the

time when you will see men in *Lederhosen* (leather pants) and women in *Dirndl* (petticoated pinafore dresses), and the *Trachtenfest* parade of beer wagons pulled by shire horses.

ANNUAL FAIRS

An important tradition in Germany is the *Messe*, or annual fair. This may be either a trade or a craft fair. The *Messe* grew out of the traditional country market where agricultural produce was exchanged, with certain areas specializing in particular produce and drawing in traders from around. There are still weekly farmers' markets in many cities. Hamburg's fish market is famous.

The *Messehalle* (trade fair hall) is a feature of many of Germany's great cities, and some of the biggest fairs are international events, such as the Frankfurt Book Fair in October, and the Hanover CeBIT computer industry trade fair in March.

For Germans a common or shared interest has always been an important reason for coming together in groups, and throughout German history there have been formations and reformations of ties between the disparate cities and states that helped them overcome to some extent the insecurity of their isolation. One such association, we have seen, was the Hanseatic League, a union of leading North Sea and Baltic coastal ports to coordinate their trading activities.

FAMILY OCCASIONS

Birthdays

In Germany, it is common on your birthday to take cakes or candy into the office to celebrate with everyone or, if at home, to keep open house that day and entertain guests. As a guest, just a handshake and congratulations are enough, but you should perhaps take a small present or flowers. Be careful not to give presents before someone's birthday—it is considered bad luck.

Weddings

The traditional stag and hen nights when bride- and groom-to-be go off separately with their friends for one last night of freedom is not observed in Germany. Instead, the couple go out together with friends for a *Polterabend*, a jolly social gathering, of which the highlight is the smashing of crockery. This doesn't mean trashing a hotel dining room or restaurant, but breaking crockery usually specially collected for just this event.

On the wedding day itself the bride might be abducted by friends of the groom for a while before the ceremony. One thing to remember is that wedding rings are worn on the third finger of the right hand, and engagement rings on the third finger of the left hand.

Familientreffen

For most people in the U.S.A. or Britain, Thanksgiving or Christmas is the time for the whole family to get together. In Germany Christmas Eve is really for the immediate family only, so *Familientreffen* (large family gatherings) once or twice a year become important occasions for meeting and catching up.

HISTORICAL CELEBRATIONS

One of the many pleasures of life in Germany is the celebration of historical events. All the way down the Rhine in summer you can enjoy *son et lumière* (historical shows using sound and light) and fireworks recalling how such and such a castle was sacked and burned. A defeat is just as much a reason for celebrating as a victory! Or, more importantly, a great celebration of deliverance, such as the passion play at Oberammergau.

Oberammergau is a phenomenon. In 1634 the plague came to the village of Oberammergau in Bavaria. The villagers prayed to God and vowed that if the community were spared they would perform a Passion every ten years in thanksgiving. It was, and they did, and the Oberammergau

Passion Play, performed every ten years since (except during the war years), has become a major cultural event. All the parts are played by the villagers, and the Passion is played out over a five-day festival. It is a remarkable and moving tribute to Oberammergau's history, sense of continuity, and sense of theater and celebration.

RELIGION IN GERMANY

There is no state religion in Germany, but some 70 percent of Germans are Christian, with a roughly fifty-fifty split between Protestants and Roman Catholics. The Germans are no more or less devout than other Europeans, but the State does subsidize the Church for certain charitable services. This subsidy takes the form of a mandatory Church tax (*Kirchensteuer*) of 4 percent of one's income. Thus whatever you may state on a form that asks for your religion, even though you may not be a churchgoer, you are liable for tax.

Christian roots are deep in Germany. Christianity was imposed when Charlemagne became Holy Roman Emperor in 800 CE, and it was reinforced by the German states' close relationship with Rome. Northeastern Germany was home to one of the most famous Christian military orders, the Teutonic Knights, who made it their crusade to convert the pagans of the Baltic region. Such was their success that knights came from all over Europe to campaign with them. The Order was disbanded when in 1525 its Grand Master converted to Protestantism.

Once Martin Luther had started the Protestant Reformation in 1517 by nailing to the door of a church in Wittenberg his objections to the excesses of the Catholic Church, Germany could well have become completely Protestant. During the Thirty Years' War between the Holy Roman Emperor and some of the Protestant states, however, the southern German states asserted their loyalty to Rome and the region has stayed predominantly Catholic ever since.

The office of Holy Roman Emperor was both religious and secular, and committed the holder to defend the interests of the Church. By the time of the Thirty Years' War the title had ceased to be elective and become the birthright of the Habsburgs. As a result the Empire came to be based on Austria and the Habsburg territories of Hungary, Bohemia, and southeastern Europe, until its abolition in 1806. The quasi-mystical significance of the Holy Roman Empire lay in its linking of the Roman Empire of antiquity, the Catholic faith, and allegiance to the Pope in Rome. For much of Germany, as opposed to Austria, however, its authority became meaningless from the sixteenth century onward.

chapter four

MAKING FRIENDS

WORK AND SOCIAL LIFE

English-speaking people find it quite easy to mix their business and social lives, to talk about their jobs at a cocktail party or mix with colleagues in a social setting. Until recently this was not the case in Germany, where business and social life were kept quite separate, and it was even considered inappropriate to discuss one's personal life at work, or work issues in a social environment. American and British people working in German companies were surprised by the way that their colleagues could work together for twenty-five years and never once address each other by their first names, or use the personal pronoun "*du*" (the intimate form of "you"), and by the fact that they might know next to nothing about each other's private lives. Things have lightened up since those days, but an element of this remains, particularly among the older generation. To people who are used to forming many of their friendships, and even romantic relationships, with colleagues at the office, this separation of work and social life can be quite frustrating, but for the Germans it is perfectly natural. Quite simply, they have another system.

Friendship means something quite special to the Germans and is not a term they use lightly. Most Germans have a small, closely knit circle of friends, and a wider network of acquaintances. Their friendships are generally formed at school and university, and are often quite local. American and British people tend to have more friends, but the relationship is often looser. For the Germans friendships are made much more slowly, but once made are closer and last for life. So it is important for visitors to Germany to recognize that friendships are not made quickly or casually, and are not formed in the office. It is also important to remember that the Germans keep private and public life separate.

So where do you meet Germans, and how do you make friends? The Germans work hard during working hours, but also play hard outside them. They are also quite fit—so sports clubs and leisure activities play a large part in many Germans' lifestyles. Gardening is very popular, and city apartment dwellers can indulge their passion in a *Schrebergarten*, or allotment garden. In all parts of Germany there are country trails with designated areas for keep-fit exercises and jogging or walking tracks. Even the Sunday afternoon walk (*Sonntagsspaziergang*) is an important habit. Outdoor activities in the summer range from football to open-air theater. There are even *Grillplätze* (barbecue points) provided in parks and woods for families and friends to hold barbecues.

Working hours in Germany are usually from 9:00 a.m. to 5:00 p.m., although most people get in to work earlier, and the lunch hour is short (sometimes as little as half an hour) and taken in the company canteen. By 4:00 p.m. the switchboard may close, and at 5:00 p.m. people will leave promptly.

The Germans are great travelers and their generous holiday entitlements encourage this. The official German working week is thirty-five to thirty-seven hours, and the general holiday entitlement is four weeks a year. It is not unusual, although it is sometimes inconvenient, for a German executive to disappear for four weeks at a time, or even to lump two years' holiday entitlement into one long vacation. Most German families with children of school age, however, are limited to taking their vacations in the school holidays. These vary from state to state but the "vacation season" is usually in July/August.

GREETINGS

A corollary of the close friend/acquaintance split in Germany is the use of greetings. American and British people are becoming more and more used to a very informal mode of greeting, with waves, nods of the head, and a casual "Hi," and often to the use of first names from the start. It is a salutary experience to realize that the Germans still maintain a degree of formality in greetings. Handshaking on arrival and departure is the norm, as is the use of surnames and even titles. In a business environment it used to be important to observe not just the title, but the *number* of titles. For example, "Herr Professor Dr. Dr. Schmidt" might be a Professor with two doctorates to his name. The procedure when meeting people is to assume formality and to ask people how they would like to be addressed if you are not sure. You will find that the younger generation of Germans are impatient with this degree of protocol and are gradually shaking it off.

The key to assessing how to address people is to know how much respect to accord them. The Germans set great store by this, and it is important not to overlook it. For the Americans, and increasingly the British, the aim is to move into an informal mode of address as quickly as possible. The Germans are happy to maintain a more formal mode of address for a much longer time into a relationship.

DU AND *SIE*

Like many other European languages German makes a distinction not just between the singular and plural pronoun "you," but between the formal and informal "you." The informal "you" is *du*, used only for family and close friends, and *Sie* for everybody else. English has no such distinction, so English-speakers using German would naturally tend to slip into the informal *du* as soon as possible. This does not happen in Germany. If you address someone by their first name and use *du* it may be seen as rude and presumptuous, although among students and now in some international companies, especially where English is the language of communication, the use of first names, even with *du*, has become acceptable. If in doubt, stay with *Sie* and the surname.

On the other hand, Germans are experts at code-switching (switching between formal and informal styles of address when foreigners are around). Among themselves, they will use the formal term and surname, yet happily switch to the informal first name and even the more intimate *du* when addressing the foreigner.

GREETINGS IN SHOPS

In spite of this formality, you will find that in shops in the west people will automatically say

"*Guten Tag*" ("Good day"), or in Bavaria "*Grüss Gott*" ("God greet you"), to everybody generally when entering the store, and "*Auf Wiedersehen*" ("Goodbye") on leaving. You should do the same.

ATTITUDES TO FOREIGNERS

On the whole the Germans are friendly and hospitable to foreigners, especially if they are tourists or on business. This does not mean that they don't appreciate your efforts to address them in German. It is well worth trying to use some German, even if only when exchanging greetings, as you will get a better response, even if you make mistakes. People who might react coolly if asked, "Do you speak English?" will respond positively in English if you are able to say in German, "*Entschuldigen Sie bitte, Sprechen Sie Englisch?*" The cautious answer will usually be, "*Ein Bisschen*" ("a bit"), but most Germans speak and understand English quite well.

The Germans today, perhaps partly in response to their past, are on the whole very courteous and open, and very concerned not to allow racism or violence against foreigners. The small outbreaks of disaffected youth attacking foreign workers and sporting right-wing or Nazi slogans are as disapproved of by their fellow Germans as they are by most foreigners.

JOINING CLUBS

The best way of making new friends in Germany is to join a club. The Germans like to pursue their leisure interests through clubs. Decide what you are interested in, then find a club that will cater for you. The local town hall or library will have a list of clubs. In major cities expatriate groups will have their own clubs, catering to foreigners and Germans alike. There are Ambassadors' clubs, American women's and men's clubs, Anglo-French clubs, International men's and women's clubs, Kiwani clubs, Lion and Lioness clubs, and Rotary clubs. You can also join the International Toastmasters. Another way of meeting people, although not Germans, is to learn German. The cheapest way of doing this is to enroll at the local German adult education college. This is called the *Volkshochschule*, or "People's" High School.

INVITATIONS HOME

The Germans are not all great home entertainers, so an invitation to someone's house may be an honor, and it is important to accept. Arriving ten to fifteen minutes late is fine, but don't be later than that. Arriving early is considered wrong. Unlike their American and British counterparts, your hosts probably won't give you a tour of the house, but the whole house will have been cleaned and tidied for your visit, the best china and cutlery laid out, and good food bought and prepared.

ENTERTAINING

Like all countries, Germany has various entertaining rituals. They may invite you to join them for *Kaffee und Kuchen* (coffee and pastries) on a Saturday or Sunday afternoon around 4.00 p.m. On these occasions guests sit down to relaxed conversations over coffee or tea and German pastries for a couple of hours.

Invitations to dinner may be earlier than you expect—6:30 p.m. or 7:00 p.m. is not uncommon— and punctuality is expected. On the other hand, it is not appreciated if you leave too early—11:00 p.m. is fine. During the meal toasts will be drunk. It is not appropriate to lift your glass until the first toast has been drunk. There is generally much raising of glasses and looking people in the eye before enjoying the wine, again a moment of formality in a convivial and relaxed atmosphere. The toast for wine is "*Zum wohl*," and for beer is "*Prost*."

After a meal guests sit around and chat. This is called *Unterhaltung*—conversational entertainment—and is an important part of the evening. If you are invited for 8:30 p.m. it may be not for a meal at all, but for after-dinner coffee and cheese.

GIFT GIVING

Many countries have elaborate gift-giving rituals. Germany does not. There is no giving of presents to colleagues, and in offices the "secret Santa," giving cards or gifts, doesn't happen. If, in the course of business, small gifts are exchanged, at the end of a successful deal, for example, they should not contain a company logo. Intimate personal gifts, such as perfume or jewelry, are not appropriate. These are for family and close friends to give. There is also a residual superstition about not giving pointed objects.

If you are invited to someone's house, it is appropriate to bring gifts for your host and hostess. Bring wine only if it is really special: Germans know their wine and have good cellars. Good quality chocolates are always acceptable, as are flowers. Avoid lilies and chrysanthemums (associated with funerals) and red roses (which are for lovers). Odd numbers are popular, but 6 and 12 are acceptable, and 13, although odd, is definitely considered unlucky. Florists abound in German cities and will happily advise you on the right sort of flowers and the right size of bouquet for any event. There is also a convention that you should unwrap the flowers before presenting them to your host and hostess and leave the paper on the hall table! Maybe an easier and more ecologically sound way of giving flowers is to present them tied together but unwrapped.

A word about wrapping gifts. Germany is a tidy-wrapping country. If you are not a proficient wrapper, get it done in the store where you buy the present. Also avoid non-biodegradable wrapping, as the Germans are very pollution-conscious.

MANNERS MAKYTH MAN

Certain social conventions, all but lost in English-speaking countries, still exist in Central Europe. Men may stand up when an important person, or women, or older people enter a room, as a mark of respect. Men may precede a woman when entering a bar or restaurant, help her with her coat, and hold the door open for her, and prefer to walk on the left-hand side when out-of-doors, or nearest to the curb. If this happens simply enjoy it as old-fashioned courtesy, not affectation.

chapter five

THE GERMANS AT HOME

Here's a strange thing. These supposedly upright, rigid, organized, and stiff Germans are relaxed and welcoming when it comes to home life. Every visitor to Germany attests to the fact that the rigid separation that the Germans make between business and personal life means that at home people are delightful, generous, excellent hosts, accommodating, and fun. How does this paradox come about?

HEIMAT

Much as in the U.S.A., less so than in Britain, and in common with other European countries, the Germans are a regional people, committed to their region and to their *Heimat*—their homeland. This is the part of the country where their parents lived, where they were brought up, where their close friends live, and perhaps where their wives, husbands, and in-laws come from.

Coming Home

A typical young couple, Achim and Constance grew up on the slopes of the hills overlooking the Rhine near Mainz. Constance's parents still have a vineyard there. Achim and Constance both work for a company in Mainz. They are sent all over the world for their company and love to travel, but eventually they want to come back and settle in Mainz. They want their children to have the same sense of belonging to their *Heimat*.

After the age of thirty or so the Germans show much less job mobility than American or British people. They prefer to seek jobs near their families in their home area. So when a leading German insurance company reduced the number of its call centers from forty-five to five, relocation was a major issue, and many of the call-center workers took voluntary layoff rather than uproot themselves and move with their company.

The German regions each have a distinctive local character. Thus Rhinelanders are renowned for generosity. The Swabians, around Stuttgart, on the other hand, are the "Scots" of Germany, known, rightly or wrongly, for thrift. The citizens of Mecklenburg in the east are considered to be reserved, and the Bavarians to be the most laid back and relaxed.

Home ownership is less common in Germany than in the rest of Europe: about 40 percent of Germans own their homes. Most people rent, and spend 25–33 percent of their net income on accommodation. Tenants enjoy considerable legal protection, and, as a result, landlords are particularly choosy about whom they accept.

German houses and apartments are well appointed, and the Germans themselves are very house proud. This extends beyond the house to its surroundings. By law, German home owners are expected to keep the adjacent sidewalks swept and free of snow, and commonly there is a rotation for apartment owners to do this.

This sense of community extends to a variety of household tasks. One is the use of communal laundry facilities. In many apartment blocks communal washing machines and driers are kept in the basement and there is a rotation system regulating their use by residents. Many residents now install their own personal equipment in their apartments, but if you are using the basement facilities and need the washing machine when it's not your day, then you have to negotiate.

Germany is one of the most ecologically aware countries in Europe and this manifests itself in garbage collection and recycling. Differently colored bags are used in recycling different types of household waste, and the appropriate bags

Communal Life

Social awareness runs deep in German home life and affects all kinds of things, such as the making of noise and the putting out of garbage. Germany's mandatory quiet hours extend from 1:00 to 3:00 p.m. and 10:00 p.m. to 7:00 a.m., Monday to Saturday and all day Sunday. You are expected not to mow your lawn, wash your car, or disturb the peace on a Sunday. By law, you can't even wash your car if it is parked in the street. You are also forbidden by law to make any excessive noise that might disturb your neighbors, such as playing loud music or using machinery, after 10:00 p.m. If you do these things, beware. Your first complaint might not be from an upset neighbor but from the police, whom your neighbors will have called. If you are having a party, let your neighbors know in advance.

need to be bought from the right municipal collection point. Some foreigners find the organization of this quite difficult to come to terms with, and it may cause rebellious feelings in those who feel that their right to choose how best to dispose of their waste is being infringed. Worst of all, the German sense of communal order is such that your neighbors may comment on your mistakes in this area, or a waste disposal team may even refuse to take waste in the wrong bag. This is definitely a case of "If you can't beat them, join them!"

Ecological awareness extends to supermarkets. "Bring your own bag" is a common practice, and the bag in question will normally be linen, not plastic. Plastic packaging is frowned upon as being nonbiodegradable and is not used in households, or by companies.

LIVING CONDITIONS

German downtown apartments may be smaller than American and British householders are used to. Many will have a dining corner in the kitchen for family or intimate meals, and a dining area in the sitting room for guest meals. The rooms may be smaller and more compact. Houses will, of course, have more and bigger rooms, and some of the traditional nineteenth- and early twentieth-century apartments, houses, and chalet-style houses in Bavaria can be very spacious indeed.

The lack of space may place a few restrictions on your lifestyle. You don't leave bicycles in hallways, for example. In fact, always keep the hallway clear, and check with your landlord about what is expected. If you're having a party, always inform your neighbors; invite them if you can. Politeness to neighbors is expected. Closeness is not. It is important not to be intrusive or overfriendly.

FURNISHING

If you decide to rent an apartment for a short time, be aware that they are unfurnished unless otherwise stated. Make sure to learn the terms used generally in advertisements. In Germany "unfurnished" means bare. The outgoing tenants usually take the light fittings and the taps. You will have a kitchen sink, bathroom equipment, light fixtures (but not necessarily fittings), and often a stove. You won't necessarily have a fridge. On the positive side, all apartments must be in mint condition when you move in, with central heating, water, and so on.

There are other costs involved apart from furnishing your new home. Rental agencies will typically demand three months' rent in advance, but will ensure that everything is done and all legal issues are taken care of (these can be complicated in Germany). You also have to pay an additional security deposit, or *Kaution*, repayable in principle on departure and usually equivalent to three months' rent.

There is also the *Nebenkosten* (utilities charges) payable to the landlord. This covers heating, but you will be responsible for gas and electricity (register with the local *Stadtwerke*, or city power generating agency) and telephones (Telekom). On the credit side, German law protecting tenants is very strong, and if you go through a rental agency it should take care of the legal side as part of the service. One important thing to remember is this: when you leave, make sure that you have fulfilled the legal requirements of the landlord, and cancel all the utilities or you could be faced with an unpleasant souvenir of your stay in Germany for a long time to come.

Central heating may be centrally controlled in apartment blocks, but you will have individual controls in your apartment. You'll also find effective window insulation in most houses as it can get very cold.

Americans constantly complain about the size of European refrigerators. Either import a Westinghouse, or be prepared to think smaller. One saving grace is that as the Germans are used to shopping for food regularly, rather than making one huge weekly excursion, there may well be two fridges, one for freezing and one for keeping food fresh.

APPLIANCES

Germany works on the metric system. This means that American and British home appliances do not conform to the German electrical system, or that your prized dining-room table may not fit into your bijou living/dining room. A lot of foreigners living in Germany prefer to buy locally and resell on departure. This is especially the case for things like fitted bed linen, as American beds, in particular, have different specifications from German ones.

German plugs are two-pronged and use 230 volts and 50 hertz. They also use PAL B system televisions. Only the plugs pose problems for the British, but Americans, with 110 volts and 60 hertz and NTSC TV systems, will have to bring adaptors, and buy their TV or video player locally. Remember that American DVDs are not compatible with European machines unless a special chip is installed. Computers should have an adaptor, but check before you leave home.

IDENTITY

All Germans carry identity cards and use them when registering children for school, at libraries, and for all kinds of registration. If you stay in Germany for under three months you can use your passport, but if you're there for longer you will need an *Aufenthaltserlaubnis*, or residence permit, and a confirmation of registration (*Anmeldebestätigung*) from the local authority.

This is proof that you live where you say you live, and all Germans have the same document. Contact the Foreign Nationals Office, or *Ausländeramt*, for details and be prepared for it to take a while. If you are American and have completed an application form before you arrive, be sure to tell the German immigration officials on arrival that you are applying for a work permit so that they don't stamp you as ineligible for work.

DAILY LIFE AND ROUTINES

The Germans tend to get up early, around 6:30 to 7:00 a.m., and would expect to be at work by 8:00 or 8:30 a.m. Families often breakfast together and, if you are staying with one, it's worth checking breakfast time with your host so that you can join them.

German breakfasts differ from traditional American or British breakfasts in the offer of bread, ham, cheese, yogurt, and muesli, as well as the customary cornflakes. There will be slices of ham, salami, or sausage, and soft-boiled eggs (but never fried food), and tea, coffee, milk, or orange juice.

Most schools start at 8:00 a.m. They are usually more local than in America and Britain. Children usually have a light lunch (sandwiches and fruit), and after-school care is slowly becoming available.

In Germany lunch is traditionally the main meal of the day and may consist of a starter followed by hot meat, fish, or vegetables, potatoes, pasta, and a salad, and a dessert of cake or fruit.

German wives and children often get together for *Kaffee und Kuchen*, the informal occasion at which coffee, tea, or soft drinks and a variety of sticky cakes and pastries are served. The aim of the afternoon is chatting and catching up, and you will be invited to sample as many of the delicacies as you can, most of which will be homemade. Do this, if only out of politeness. Many guests take a small gift of food (American cookies and shortbread are popular).

Children return from school around 4:00 p.m. (earlier, of course, for primary schools), and the evening meal, a lighter meal of cold meats, fish, and cheese is served with bread or rolls. Beer, cider, wine, and sometimes herbal tea, may be taken with these meals. Supper is usually early— between 6:00 and 6:30 p.m.—but if guests have been invited it will be at 7:30 or 8:00 p.m. People generally go to bed early during the week, at 10:30 to 11:00 p.m.

BOUNDS AND BOUNDARIES

German houses are more like British houses than American. Clear boundary divisions act as a protection against the outside. Fences and borders are well kept and psychologically well defended. The same goes for inside. In some countries you can expect "the tour of the house" on your first visit, which helps to create a relaxed, informal atmosphere. You may even ask "Can I help?" and wander into the kitchen to chat to your hostess. This is rare in Germany, where things are a little more formal. The atmosphere will be relaxed and friendly, but the whole house, although clean and sparkling, is not open to visitors.

The layout of the average German house or apartment reflects this sense of order and boundaries. On entering, you will find not an open-plan living area but a small closed corridor. Off this open the rooms of the house, the doors of which are normally closed. This is partly an economy measure. Rooms in German households are often individually heated, so a closed door keeps the heat inside. Your strategy: don't ask to see the house unless your relations with the host encourage it, and don't go into the kitchen unless you know you will be welcomed. Your respect for German privacy will earn their respect and affection in turn, and open doors that might otherwise remain closed.

"*KINDER, KÜCHE, KIRCHE*" ("CHILDREN, KITCHEN, CHURCH")

This phrase is often now used mockingly, to describe the traditional and conservative role of the German mother. As in other Western countries, the role of women in business and in the home has changed quite radically as more and more women have full-time jobs. The traditional role of the *Hausfrau* (housewife) who looked after the home, the children, and the old people in the family is now a matter of taste rather than of necessity. However, there are significant differences in this regard between East and West Germany. In the former Eastern states women had a lot of state support, including free child-care facilities. With reunification, that has gone and there are much higher unemployment levels among women in the East. Where women do choose to forgo careers and to make bringing up their children their business, they are accorded a good deal of respect. There is still a significant debate in Germany about whether or not women should work full time, while more and more women are actually both working full time, in offices and factories, and running their households.

SCHOOLS AND SCHOOLING

In any household with children school plays an important part, and it is a good idea to take an intelligent interest in your neighbor's or friend's children's education. All German children attend school from six to eighteen, although most go first to Kindergarten from the age of three. From six to ten (or twelve in Berlin) children attend the *Grundschule* (elementary or primary school). The two years from eleven to twelve, or thirteen to fourteen, are important to German children because they are the *Orientierungsstufe*, or orientation stage, where children are assessed prior to undertaking a more focused course of study. After this they may enter the academic stream (*Gymnasium*) and proceed toward the academic school-leaving examination at eighteen, called the *Abitur*. Something like 35 percent of German school students go to *Gymnasium*. Twenty percent of German children attend a vocationally oriented *Realschule*, where they receive core educational teaching but with a strong practical element. Some students will move across into *Gymnasium*, but most will graduate with a diploma that will qualify them for entry into a commercial or technical college.

A further 25 percent of students attend *Hauptschule*, or general high school. Once again, the emphasis is on core education with a vocational bias. Students will graduate with a diploma enabling them to attend a *Berufsschule* (vocational school). This system ensures that Germany has a supply of support staff with a good general and vocational level of education.

The final type of secondary school is the *Gesamtschule*, or comprehensive school, which offers a mixture of academic, commercial, and vocational programs and is an attempt to break down the social stratification that can result from dividing children into academic and vocational streams.

German schools are run by the individual *Länder*, so there are differences between the sixteen state educational systems, and education is free. Private schools exist but are in a minority.

Alternative systems include religious schools, which have the same curriculum as state scools, but stress their own particular values; Waldorf schools, based on the philosophy of Rudolf Steiner, which emphasisize creativity; and Montessori schools.

If you know a family with young children, remember that the first day of school is a big rite of passage, marked by the giving of the *Schultüte*.

The most obvious difference in education between the United States and Germany is that the Germans specialize much earlier than the Americans. They are being groomed for a fairly specific job market from the ages of twelve to fourteen, and the education system is still quite "top down" and monitored by regular standardized tests. American and British education at elementary and secondary/high-school level has developed many more "student centered" education options, with continuous assessment, group project work, and so on. Increased individualism among German students has created demands for a less directive system, and is the subject of some debate among German parents and educational theorists.

TV AND RADIO

One of the pleasures of being in the center of Europe is that you receive programs from all over the Continent. The German satellite television  system will get you programming from Germany, Spain, Italy, and Turkey, as well as CNN, Eurosport, and other international channels. Most houses and apartment blocks are wired for satellite.

Germany works on the PAL-B/G system. This is different from the American NTSC and the British PAL systems. You can play PAL video cassettes, but the British may experience problems with transmission if they take their own TVs. The recommendation is to buy local.

Unlike the practice in many countries, German television programs are all broadcast in German. This means that (mainly) US television series and films are dubbed into German. Unless you like watching *Friends* in German, look for a set that has a switch to allow you to hear the original language track, not the dubbed track.

Without satellite reception or cable TV, German television is quite limited. There are three public broadcasters, ARD, ZDF, and a network of regional stations, all of which enjoy national reception and some of which duplicate each other's programming.

In many countries one pays for a single license that covers all the radio and television sets in the house. The Germans pay an annual license fee on each radio or TV set they use. Register through the *Gebühreneinzugszentrale*, or GEZ (fee payment office).

If you watch German TV or go into a news agency the provision of sexually explicit material is quite open. The Germans are not at all prudish about sex and treat it quite matter-of-factly. What will upset them is not sex but violence. Therefore some of the videos or movies you might think of as unexceptional will be viewed very badly by the Germans, whereas programs that you might find unacceptable for viewing by, say, young teenagers will be perfectly acceptable in German households.

There is a viewer's guidance system in Germany for feature films, called the *Freiwillige Selbstkontrolle*, with five categories. These are: *Ohne alterbeschränkung* (no limit), *ab 6 jahre*, *ab 12 jahre*, *ab 16 jahre*, and *ab 18 jahre* (suitable from 6, 12, 16, and 18 years old).

COMPLAINING

Speaking Your Mind

Late at night at a German airport the German taxi driver packed five disparate plane passengers into his cab to take them to their different hotels. After all, he explained, it was better to suffer a bit of discomfort and get to the hotel quickly than to wait to be ferried individually. "And it can't be so bad for you either," piped up one German passenger, "as you're charging full fares." "How German!" the non-Germans all sighed, "How discourteous!"

Even though what she was saying was probably true, the other passengers felt the driver should more properly have been thanked for his willingness to bend the rules. Germans, however, are never slow to tell it as they see it and don't understand the British and, to some extent, American reluctance to quibble.

Be prepared for the Germans to be forthright about bad service, high rents, or unacceptable behavior, and to voice their opinions in general. If someone complains to you, develop a thick skin, and if you are a complainer yourself remember there is a difference between being frank and being tactless. Above all, don't complain that you are among a nation of whiners. You are not.

ARE YOU *STAMMTISCH?*

Ask people what the center of the household is, and you'll get different answers. For most it's the living room, for some the bedroom, for some the terrace, for many the kitchen. For the Germans it's around a table, talking. The table, be it in the living room or in the kitchen, is the place where life and communication happen. Germans still prefer to sit and talk around a table, time permitting, than to watch TV.

As in the home so it is outside. Germany is very much a pub culture. People go to drink and socialize in beer gardens and beer halls, where they sit around tables, sometimes as whole families, and drink and talk—and sing. It is a popular and recognized meeting point.

Stammtisch is a word that you should learn. German pubs and beer halls often have a table that is set aside for regular clients. If you as a stranger sit at it, you may be asked politely to move because you aren't *Stammtisch*—regular at the table. In a German household you'll know that you are really part of the furniture when, instead of relaxing in the deep, comfortable chairs of the living room, you are huddled round a table in the kitchen or living room on a hard chair, a drink in your hand, arguing about the issues of the day. Don't be surprised if, when invited to dinner, you find yourself sitting around the table for an hour after dinner is over, happily chatting over coffee or drinks.

CHANGING LIFE STYLES

You may remember the old joke that in America and Britain everything is permitted except what is expressly forbidden, and that in Germany everything is forbidden that is not expressly permitted. Reading this chapter you may begin to feel that that is actually the case. It's important to remember that for the Germans an ordered society makes for a better, easier, and more productive life for everyone. Therefore they are prepared to put up with what might be seen as petty restrictions on personal liberty for the greater good, both personal and social. Foreigners living and working in Germany quickly get used to the lifestyle and, on repatriation, often rail against the "anarchy" of the society they have returned to.

However, in Germany things are changing, and there is increased individualism and rebellion against the ordered society. Like the rest of Western Europe, there is a significant rise in the number of people living together without getting married, and of single-parent families. There are also communal living arrangements, called *Wohngemeinschaften*, where people live together in a community trust.

As lifestyles change so do the attitudes of children. School and parents raise each child to be independent, self-reliant, and, above all, a responsible citizen (*mündiger Bür*ger) who will be politically aware and who will ask questions and expect answers. University students today are far less accepting of the old educational conventions. Following on from the generation that pulled down the Berlin Wall, young people are still overturning a number of the precepts their parents live by and moving toward a more individualistic and libertarian lifestyle.

For foreigners living or visiting Germany, for every "traditional" German you meet there will be one who is rebelling against the ordering of society, looking for new ideas, new thinking, and new ways of doing things. It makes for an intellectually adventurous and exciting mix.

chapter six

TIME OUT

The Germans benefit from quite a lot of time off, in addition to a working week of thirty-seven hours, or even less in some places.

On the whole people don't work overtime and most offices close at 5:00 p.m. As we have seen, they have up to fifteen legal holidays a year and, like other countries, if a holiday falls on a Thursday then people often make a bridge and do not return to work on the Friday.

German annual vacations are generous by any standards. They are a minimum of four weeks, and can extend to six weeks for senior executives. May and June are popular vacation times, as are July and August.

Sickness and maternity benefits are also generous. Mothers have up to six weeks' paid leave before the birth of their child, and up to eight weeks' afterward. Workers are entitled to up to six weeks' fully paid sick leave, and can even claim a regular visit to a *Kur* or health spa on the basis of medical advice. "Going on *Kur*" is not uncommon in German firms. So how do the Germans fill all this free time?

SHOPPING

The Germans shop as much for leisure as for
sustenance. Shopping in Germany differs to some
extent from shopping in the U.S.A. and the U.K.
in that there is much greater use of local specialty
stores and less reliance on supermarkets. This is

Bakery *(Bäckerei)*
Fresh bread, rolls, pretzels, and pizzas.
Often open very early in the morning.

Butcher *(Metzgerei or Fleischerei)*
Fresh and cooked meat and sausages.

Grocery Store *(Lebensmittelgeschäft)*
A range of groceries.

Greengrocer *(Obst- und Gemüseladen)*
Fruit and vegetables.

Chemist or Pharmacy *(Apotheke)*
Pharmaceutical products are sold in two stores. The *Drogerie*
sells cosmetics and hygiene products, whereas the *Apotheke*
is a dispensing chemist, offering medicine. Pharmacists can
recommend medicine, and there is a weekend rotation
system to make sure a pharmacy is always open to fulfill
urgent prescriptions.

---

because German cooks still prefer to buy fresh
local ingredients rather than prepackaged ones.
Supermärkte there are, of course, but the specialty
shops are far more interesting. The Germans, like
the Italians, value the quality of fresh food and
appreciate seasonal variety.

In most towns every week there is a market, usually advertised in the local newspaper, held in the city center. These sell fresh flowers, meat, fish, and vegetables. Unlike in France or Italy you are not encouraged to pick up and squeeze fruit before purchase.

The Germans, as you would expect, are orderly shoppers who wait in line and observe the order of service. What surprises many foreigners is that the Germans treat a shop, although not a supermarket or department store, as a communal space and will expect to greet everybody as they enter with a general "*Guten Morgen*" or "*Guten Tag*," or in the south with "*Grüss Gott.*" As a foreigner you are not expected to follow suit, although as you feel more part of the community you will find it a friendly and neighborly thing to do.

The Germans like to get the products, prices, and change right, and will ask persistent questions to make sure they get precisely what they want, or are given exactly the right change. This may take a little time. The marked price includes tax.

SUNDAY CLOSING

During the week shops open at around 8:00 or
9:00 a.m. and close at 8:00 p.m. One thing that
surprises many visitors is weekend shop closing.
On Saturday, shops can stay open until 6:00 p.m.,
but may close earlier. On Sunday, not only shops
but supermarkets in or near large cities are closed.
Bakeries, however, may be open for a few hours,
for those fresh rolls for breakfast that the
Germans are so fond of. Otherwise, the only
shops open on Sunday are twenty-four-hour gas
stations. On the four days before Christmas shops
remain open until 6:00 p.m.

BANKS

Banks in Germany are open from 8:30 a.m. to
4:00 p.m., and some stay open till 5:30 p.m. on
Thursdays. Some small banks may close for lunch
between 1:00 and 2:30 p.m. Banks are not open
on Saturdays.

Germany is part of the Eurozone and the old
currency, the Deutschmark, has now been replaced
by the Euro. Other traditions don't change, however.
This is still a cash-driven society, and not all
restaurants and stores even accept credit cards as
payment. One British manager said he used as many
checks in a year in Germany as he used in a month
in Britain. Most Germans have a *Girokonto* (current

or checking account) and a *Sparkonto* (savings account). Bills are paid from the *Girokonto*. People who come to your house to provide cleaning, delivery, or repair services may simply give you the bill with their giro number and ask you to make a direct payment into their account. Standing orders (*Daueraufträge*) are used for regular payments such as rent; direct debits (*Lastschriftverfahren*) for utilities; and transfers (*Überweisungen*) for one-off payments. There is increasing use of online banking.

The average German doesn't use personal checks but may occasionally use Eurochecks, which are a kind of traveler's check. Where plastic is used it will be a debit rather than a credit card owing to the German aversion to credit. Germans much prefer to pay out of their income, and if they don't have the money, to hold off the purchase until they do. ATMs, called *Geldautomaten*, are available in all cities and Cirrus, Visa, and Plus systems are usually accepted.

RESTAURANTS, FOOD AND DRINK

Where will you find some of the best Italian cooking outside Italy? Try Frankfurt/Main. Major German cities have become centers of multicultural cuisine, thanks largely to Germans traveling worldwide and acquiring a taste for foreign cooking. Where, however, do you go for German cooking?

The first thing to say is that the standard of cooking generally is good, tasty, reasonably healthy, and clean. The Germans pride themselves on fresh, high-quality food. Pork is the most commonly eaten meat, and vegetarian food is easy to find. Like most nationalities, the Germans are subject to food stereotypes: if the British eat fish and chips, and the Americans hamburgers, then the Germans eat nothing but sauerkraut and sausage. It's true that they consume an astonishing variety of sausages, but there is also venison, boar, quail, and duck, as well as a wide variety of seafood in the north and east.

It is unusual to get a bad meal or snack in Germany, although not impossible. For food on the run, the Germans go to a *Stehimbiss* or *Schnellimbiss* (snack bar). These are places where you eat standing up or buy food to take away, and they serve *Fritten* or *Pommes* (French fries) or *Kartoffelsalat* (potato salad), *Bratwurst* (sausage), and maybe kebabs. These snack bars are frequently owned by chains such as Nordsee (specializing in fish), Wienerwald (specializing in chicken), or McDonalds.

To try regional cooking, go to a typical German *Gasthaus* or *Gasthof* (inn). These will serve regional and local dishes, maybe fish in the north and dumplings (*Knöd*el) in the south.

Most of the restaurants that you are likely to go into will have menus in both German and English, or the waiters will usually be able to explain in English what the dishes are. Many restaurants, especially family-owned ones, close one day a week, usually on Monday.

Drink

Beer is by far the best-known German drink. Although lager is often thought of as the classic German beer, there is actually a wide variety of different types. There are over 1,500 breweries in Germany. In Cologne you can try a *Kölsch*, in Düsseldorf an *Alt*. In the south you can find *Weizenbier,* and in the east different kinds of *Pils*.

Germany makes wine, too, of course, especially the fine white wines traditionally known as Hocks and Moselles. You can find crisp, elegant Riesling wines from the Mosel valley, and distinctive flinty Franconian wines from northern Bavaria. The major wine-producing region is the Palatinate (Rheinpfalz, or Pfalz, in German), just north of Alsace, that produces full-bodied grapey wines. In choosing a wine remember the words *süss* and

TYPES OF GERMAN BEER

Alt or Altbier
"Old," top-fermented red-brown beer fairly close to an English ale.

Dunkel
Dark beer (from roasting the malt). The *Dunkel* category includes "dark lagers" and dark wheat beers.

Hefeweizen, Weissbier, or Weisse
Wheat beer, bottle-conditioned (*hefe* = yeast) so that it's slightly cloudy with sediment. *Weissbier* has a characteristic fruity "bubble-gum" flavor.

Kristal or Kristallweizen
Wheat beer filtered to remove the sediment.

Lager
German for "store." Lager is slowly fermented by bottom-fermenting yeast. Originally a dark Munich style. Pale *Pilsener* lagers predominate now.

Pils or Pilsener
A classic pale lager style developed in the nineteenth century at Pilsen to give a very clear, clean-tasting beer.

Kölsch
A style from Köln (Cologne), not a lager, but a pale golden top-fermented ale. Other useful beer terminology is: *hell* or *helles* = light-colored; *Roggen* = rye; *Kloster* = cloister (beer originally brewed in a convent or monastery).

Berliner Weisse
A top-fermented, bottle-conditioned wheat beer made with both traditional warm-fermenting yeasts and lactobacillus culture. It has a rapidly vanishing head and a clear, pale golden straw-colored appearance. The taste is refreshing, tart, sour, and acidic, with a lemony citric fruit sharpness and almost no hop bitterness. Berliners often add woodruff or raspberry syrup to reduce the sharpness and acidity of the beer—in fact you are almost certain to be asked "red or green" when ordering one—but they are well worth trying without additions. Berliners also tend to drink it through a straw, which is certainly not the way to get the most from a beer. With food, *Berliner Weisse* would make a good aperitif and it might go well with cheeses and salads.

lieblich (sweet), and *trocken* (dry).
German wines come in
different categories of
quality. You have the
everyday, perfectly
acceptable *Tafelwein* (table
wine), the officially tested
Qualitätswein (quality wine),
or the *Qualitätswein mit
Prädikat* (particularly fine wine).

Germany has excellent fruit juices (*Orangesaft*,
Apfelsaft), but most Germans drink bottled water,
even at home. Drinks are usually served without
ice, or, if with ice, just a cube or two. You can ask
for plain water (*ohne Kohlensäure*), but it isn't
always available.

Restaurant Etiquette
On the whole you are served at a table, even in a
pub. The ubiquitous beer mat is used to keep
track of the number of drinks you've had. In
some parts of Germany a glass of water
accompanying coffee, tea, or alcoholic drinks
performs the same function.

It is interesting to note that while table
manners in Germany are much the same as in
America and Britain, the Germans tend to be
more punctilious about table settings and don't
on the whole like "finger food."

Roughly half of the country's breweries are in Bavaria, and Munich is its beer capital. Locally made beer is drunk in the brewery's beer garden (*Biergarten*) at wooden tables without tablecloths where, by tradition, you can bring your own food and eat under the chestnut trees, as long as you buy the beer. Traditionally the beer garden is situated above the cellars, with the trees planted to keep the beer cool. The winter equivalent is the *Bierkeller* (beer cellar, below ground) or *Bierhalle* (beer hall, above ground) where people sit at long tables and drink beer. A tradition of drinking songs has grown up from this communal activity. The other popular German drinking place is the *Bierstube*, or pub.

The word for "cheers" in German is *Prost*, pronounced "proast." A beer drinker will raise his or her glass, say "*Prost*," and then clink glasses with you. Drinking takes place over a period of time and is accompanied by substantial snacks, so people get "merry" and "tipsy" rather than violently drunk. Of course, the very tight drink-driving laws ensure that fewer people take the risk of drinking and driving.

Before eating people will normally say "*Guten Appetit*" (literally, "Good appetite") and you can reply "*Guten Appetit*" or "*Danke, ebenfalls*" ("Thanks. You too."). It's worth remembering if you are American that, like the British, the

Germans tend to keep both utensils in their hands when eating, and do not first cut their food up and then eat it with a fork in the right hand. The Germans also use special fish knives when eating fish. Don't cut dumplings and vegetables with your knife as this suggests they are underdone. Chewing with the mouth open and speaking while you are eating is considered bad manners—as, by the way, is chewing gum.

In some popular establishments where there is no booking people sometimes share tables. You may find yourself seated on a long bench sharing with others at the equally long table. This is especially typical of beer halls. If you hear a sudden yelp or bark coming from under a table, don't worry. Owners' pet dogs are welcome in most of the restaurants. You will find that people smoke more than in America or Britain.

Waiters and Waitresses

To get the attention of the waiter or waitress raise your hand and, if necessary, call "Waiter" ("*Herr Ober*") or "Waitress" ("*Fräulein*"). When getting the bill (*die Rechnung*), if you need a receipt, ask for a *Quittung*. It is quite common to get separate bills if you are in a group, but let the waiter or waitress know beforehand.

Tipping
Service is included in restaurant bills by law, so the leaving of tips is a personal gift for good service. Most Germans simply round up the bill to the nearest Euro and ask for their change less the tip. This extra tip is known as *Trinkgeld* (drink money). German waiters do not depend on tips to augment their salary so, if you are tipping more formally in an expensive restaurant, 10 percent is normal.

LEISURE
No it's not just Lederhosen, Dirndl, Steins brimming with beer, and "oompah oompah" bands. There is a huge variety of activities that Germans get involved in, both indoor and outdoor.

Finding Out What's Available
Most German cities have a tourist office and actively recommend and promote places to go and things to see and do.

There is a wide variety of accommodation in Germany, all of it clean and functioning, from five-star hotels to caravans. These are described on page 122-3.

Festivals and Theme Parks

We have already mentioned the great German festivals, but every town or village has its annual festival and it's worth seeking them out. You'll also find a number of theme parks that provide wonderful days out for children, such as Phantasialand, near Cologne, or Warner Brothers' Movie World, near Essen.

HIGH CULTURE

Germany is richer in museums than most other countries. It is said that any town with a population of more than 10,000 has at least two museums, and Berlin alone has over a hundred. This plethora points up the intelligent interest that the Germans take in their own culture. There is a general awareness of and an active interest in high culture that is hard to find elsewhere.

This is particularly evident in Germany's theater and opera tradition. This is a legacy of the time when the country was divided into independent principalities and each principality vied for the best court composers and orchestras.

German-speaking composers such as Mozart, J. S.
Bach, Beethoven, and Haydn, whether German or
Austrian, all benefited from this patronage of the
arts, which continues to this day in the form of
generous Federal Government subsidies. The
result is some of the best orchestras in the world,
of which perhaps the most famous are the Berlin
Philharmonic—raised to eminence under the
magisterial postwar baton of Herbert von
Karajan, and before him by Wilhelm Furtwängler
and Arturo Toscanini—and the Leipziger
Gewandhaus, whose former director, Kurt Masur,
now works in the U.S.A.

   As well as classical opera, orchestral concerts,
and ballet, there is a thriving German Rock,
jazz, and blues scene that gets little publicity
outside Germany itself.

The heavy local subsidies for German opera and theater mean that prices are reasonable and everybody can go. There is a very wide audience from all strata of society, although maybe not so much the young. Dress for opera and theater can vary from tuxedo and evening dress to smart casual. It seems that in Germany the gap between "high" and popular culture is less pronounced than in other parts of Europe. This is due largely to the strong support given by the state to the performing arts and the drive to make them accessible to more people. But it may also be due to the German education system, which inculcates a serious approach to art and culture.

POPULAR CULTURE

Most people have heard of the Reeperbahn and of the clubs and bars of St. Pauli in Hamburg, where the Beatles began to make their name in the late 1950s before exploding on to the international scene in Britain and America between 1962 and 1964. They probably haven't heard of the bars and discos and Germany's own "techno" music in the larger towns.

The Germans are among the most tolerant of European nations to the public expression of sexual activity, both gay and heterosexual. Berlin has a flourishing gay scene, and its famous Love Parade is one big techno party. One of the more startling social amenities are the "love hotels," sometimes with neon-lit hearts above them, offering meeting places for lovers.

COUNTRYSIDE PURSUITS

We have already seen that one of the first things to strike visitors flying into German cities, even Berlin and Frankfurt/Main, is the large area of green surrounding them. These forest areas allow the city and its people to breathe, and local councils rent out forest huts to families wishing to hold barbecues or parties in the countryside. Hiking and walking, especially in groups, are popular weekend activities, as is cycling.

SPORT

Organized sport and fitness has a long history in Germany. It was introduced into German education during the wars against Napoleon between 1797 and 1815 as a way of ensuring fitness prior to military training. At the beginning of the twentieth century the *Turn- und Sportsverstände* (gym and sports) movement sprang up in Germany, and became very popular. Many of Germany's sports clubs and associations date from this time, and in the United States the *Turnverein*, or gymnastics club, is part of the German-American tradition. In the 1920s the *Wandervögel* (literally, "birds of passage") youth movement swept the country, promoting closeness to nature, outdoor activities, especially hiking, and folk culture. Unfortunately these wholesome and idealistic movements were superseded by enforced membership of the Hitler Youth in the 1930s. Leni Riefenstahl's famous propaganda documentary about the Olympic Games in Munich in 1936 is a paean to physical perfection. After the Second World War, Communist East Germany, too, made a fetish of physical fitness, using its sporting achievements to bolster the regime.

Today the Germans continue to be sports enthusiasts. Nobody needs reminding of the achievement of German soccer teams, both in Europe and in the World Cup, and German

stars have become world
celebrities. But the Germans
are equally crazy about
tennis, handball,
basketball, shooting,
riding, hockey,
cycling, Formula One
motor racing, and
many other sports.

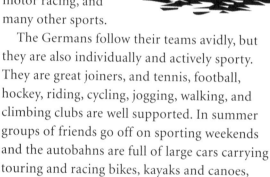

The Germans follow their teams avidly, but
they are also individually and actively sporty.
They are great joiners, and tennis, football,
hockey, riding, cycling, jogging, walking, and
climbing clubs are well supported. In summer
groups of friends go off on sporting weekends
and the autobahns are full of large cars carrying
touring and racing bikes, kayaks and canoes,
skis and boats.

TRAVELING

You're on the autobahn, you're driving along, enjoying the scenery at 70 miles an hour. You glance in your rearview mirror: nothing else on the road. Suddenly a Mercedes or BMW screams past you at 120 miles an hour. Where did that come from? Here's your first lesson. Germany's autobahns are excellent, fast, and there are stretches that have no speed limit. German auto engineering and German drivers take full advantage of this. No problem, as long as you don't hog the outside (left-hand) lane, and do check your mirror. However, it's worth remembering that if you are involved in a high-speed collision, and survive, you could lose your driver's license, even if it's not your fault.

Cars in Germany, even more than in the U.S.A., are a status symbol and it is important that your car be clean, well maintained, and in good condition. The TÜV, or *Technischer Überwachungsverein*, is responsible for inspecting all vehicles more than three years old, and they carry out the tests with extreme rigor.

Private motoring in Germany is a joy, and public transport both works and is accessible. In Germany, if a train is four minutes late the people on the platform mutter that the country is going to the dogs. In Britain, if a train is four minutes late they breathe a sigh of relief that, for once, it is on time. In Germany, public transport and services are expected to work. An interesting feature of German industry is that small and medium-sized businesses are frequently situated in far-flung outer suburbs, miles away from the main city centers. That they can function there at all is entirely due to the country's efficient public transport network.

German cities have a variety of public transport systems ranging from trams and buses to trains and subways. By and large the system is fast, efficient, and, above all, coordinated. The quality of the transportation network is in one respect a tribute to the German sense of order. It's a standard joke that you can set your watch by the departure and arrival times of German trains, but the principle behind it is that lateness is sloppy and lacking in respect.

ROAD SENSE IN GERMANY

- The Germans are good on control.
  So where speed limits are in force, expect
  radar checks.

- Traffic buildup starts early in big cities.
  Expect serious congestion as early as 7 a.m.
  and plan accordingly.

- School vacations cause chaos on the roads in
  terms of gridlock around major cities. Be
  prepared!

- If there are no signs saying otherwise, traffic
  coming from the right has right-of-way.

- Cyclists are common in towns. They are
  regarded as road users who have equal rights
  with motorized traffic. Most towns have
  cycle paths running alongside the roads and
  if you are turning right across a cycle track,
  the cyclist has right-of-way.

- In German towns and cities marked
  pedestrian crossings are guides rather than
  legally enforceable stops. Be prepared for the
  possibility that if you stop for pedestrians
  the car behind you might not! Check your
  rearview mirror before stopping.

- On the other hand, German drivers will
  usually stop for pedestrians who are crossing
  the road in narrow side streets or exits.

- Trams or streetcars are common in many German cities. If you are behind a tram when it stops, by law you must wait until all passengers have gotten off and cleared the street. Don't try to pass it.

- In former East Germany, and less often in West Germany, you may see green arrows at traffic lights, allowing you to turn right although the lights are red. This only applies to right turns where the turn does not interfere with oncoming traffic.

- All persons in the car, front and back, must wear a seatbelt. Children under the age of twelve require a special seatbelt.

- A German car blinking its lights at you on the autobahn from behind is not saying "Hello." It's telling you to get out of the way fast!

- Germans know their highway codes and road signs (the result of extensive written and oral tests). If you are doing more than just passing through Germany as a tourist, you should, too.

GETTING CAUGHT

The police are very strict about enforcing the traffic laws, and the fines are heavy. This extends from parking fines to road accidents. If you park on a cycle track or obstruct other vehicles, you may find that your car has been towed away. The police will tell you where to go and how much you have to pay to retrieve it.

By law you have to carry your travel documents in the car and also to keep a red and white warning triangle in the trunk of the car for use in case of accidents, to warn the traffic behind you that you are immobile. German drivers also have to carry a first aid kit, pass basic first aid courses, and are by law expected to administer first aid if required.

Even in less serious accidents it is usually a good idea to advise the police. You should make a note of the other driver's car registration number, name, and address and, if possible, the name of the insurance company. It is customary for drivers to exchange car documents in order to verify this information. Obviously, where possible, it is a good idea to get names and addresses of witnesses.

If you are caught speeding you can pay cash on the spot or be sent the fine in the mail. In that case, you will receive a bank transfer form with the fine on it to take or send to your bank for payment.

DRINKING AND DRIVING

The alcohol restrictions are very tight in Germany, and strictly applied. Random breath tests are not uncommon. You are only allowed 0.5 promille—an alcohol level of 50 milligrams, equal to a limit of 0.05 percent or 0.5 grams per liter of blood. It is possible to reach this level after just one beer. If you are invited out to dinner, your hosts will be very aware of this restriction and will be concerned about your driving if you are running the risk of being "over the limit."

CAR AND DRIVER'S LICENSES

These are issued at the *Kraftfahrzeugsamt* (KFZ-Amt). Contact your local office for any questions about licensing or driver's permits. If you are from the U.S.A., Canada, or the U.K., you can drive for up to a year in Germany on your existing license or an international driver's license. However, any non-German license must be accompanied by a translation into German. This you can get from the local ADAC (*Allgemeine Deutscher*

Automobilclub), which is the equivalent of the AAA in the U.S.A. or the AA in the U.K.

After six months you will need a German driver's license. Obtain this before the time is up. EU members can simply change their national license for a German one. Some American states have reciprocal arrangements with Germany that allow them to do the same, but if your state doesn't, you will have to go to a *Fahrschule* (driving school) and take a first aid course. To get a driver's license you need your application form, a residence permit, two passport photos, your current driver's permit, its translation into German, your driving school certificate, your first aid course certificate—oh, and the results of a vision test. All these should be taken to the local police station for processing.

JAYWALKING

Americans will find walking around in Germany easier than British people, as they are used to waiting at crossings. Germans do not jaywalk, even if the crossing is empty of traffic. They tend to wait for the green light. Your failure to do so will result in other pedestrians reprimanding you or even a fine from an on-duty policeman.

In Germany, pedestrian crossings are for guidance to traffic rather than a rule. Once again, vistors used to enforcing their rights to cross at a marked crossing might be taken aback. Check that the road is clear before crossing!

TRAINS

The public transport network is extensive, with first- and second-class rail travel available. The German railway system is known as the *Deutsche Bahn* (German Rail), or DB. There are hourly express trains between major cities called ICE, or IC, and sometimes on express trains you may have to pay a supplement for short journeys of less than 31 miles (50 kilometers).

Some trains that specialize in business transport (for example, to trade fairs) have first-class seats only. Tickets are usually checked on the train rather than at the station, but at many stations you are expected to revalidate your ticket before boarding by sticking it into a punch machine on the platform. Destinations, times, and platforms are well posted in German using the 24-hour clock and the name of the destination.

If you're going on a long journey, it's worth reserving your seat in advance, by contacting a travel agent showing the DB sign. Staff will usually speak English. Avoid sitting in a seat reserved by someone else (marked *reserviert*) unless you are alighting before the person is due to board the train.

You can buy a ticket from the conductor on the train, but there is a surcharge for doing so. If you travel frequently, it is a good idea to purchase a *Bahnkarte* (available for individuals and families), after which any ticket you buy is halved in price. A *Bahnkarte* can quickly pay for itself. In "Green" circles it's a must. The *Bahnkarte* is only one of a variety of cut-price tickets available. A *Schönes-Wochenendticket* ("happy weekend ticket") includes unlimited travel on local lines, and *Guten Abend* ("good evening") tickets offer off-peak reductions.

Two tickets you should know about must be purchased outside Germany. These are the German rail pass, allowing unlimited travel for a set number of four to ten days, and the Eurail pass, which gives unlimited travel in seventeen European countries. Enquire about these at your local travel agent. It's worth noting that a door-to-door service exists for baggage. Check this out at your local station.

LOCAL TRANSPORT—
BUS AND TRAM SERVICES

In Germany most towns have a bus or trolley car service (*Strassenbahn*, or *S-Bahn*), and sometimes both. There are good regional and rural bus services connecting villages to the train network. In big cities there are also subway systems called

Untergrundbahn, or *U-Bahn*. Tickets are bought from machines. Instructions are always in German, and the system is sometimes difficult to work out. Ask a passer-by for help.

There are two types of bus system, one run by German rail and one by the city. Generally the timetables of the rail and streetcar systems are well coordinated.

Some bus drivers accept payment on the bus, but be prepared for the fact that you may be expected to have bought your ticket at a kiosk or tobacconist *before* you board the bus. You then punch your ticket into a machine on the bus or streetcar to validate it for that journey. Germans trust you to buy and validate your tickets. However, if an inspector boards and you are found not to have done so, expect a significant fine. All-night bus services are rare in Germany. You should check first and last bus times.

TAXIS

Available taxis show an illuminated sign in capital letters on top of the cab. They can be hailed in the street or at a cab stand, or phoned at their headquarters. Fares are shown on the meter and tipping is not expected, although business people often "round up" the fare by one or two Euros. There may be a small supplement for luggage and dogs.

STAYING IN GERMANY

Breathe a sigh of relief. Wherever you go in Germany, no matter how simple the accommodation, the hotels will be clean and efficient, with hot water showers that work. The Germans expect quality and efficiency, and by and large they get it.

German hotels are characterized by five grades or stars, each grade offering a specific number and type of facilities. *Gasthäuser* (hotels) are quite expensive, but *Hotels garnis* (bed and breakfast) or *Gasthöfe* (bars with rooms) are more reasonable. *Pensionen*, which give a minimal breakfast, are cheaper still. These are often family run and can be quite individual and charming. The sign *Zimmer Frei* means rooms are available.

There are plenty of youth hostels, and rooms in private houses, or even apartments with kitchenettes. The local tourist office, often in the main station, or *Bahnhof*, can be very helpful, giving accommodation advice to match your needs and also making the booking for you. There is a national hotel booking agency: ADZ Room Reservation Service, Corneliusstr. 34, D-60325 Frankfurt-am-Main (tel. 069 74 767). Alternatively, you can try the *Michelin Red Guide Germany 2002*, or *The Main Cities of Europe*, also published by Michelin.

The Germans are great travelers, and there are over 2,000 official campsites for tents and caravans as well the most extensive network of youth hostels in Europe. Rules and opening times vary, but for information try your German National Tourist Office or the German Camping Club (DDC, Mandlstr. 28, D80802 Munich, tel. 089 380 14 20) or website: www.campingclub.de. Youth hostels are run by the German Youth Hostel Association (*Deutsches Jugendherbergswerk*, or DJH), and you have to be a member of the International Youth Hostel Association (IYHA) to enter them. The DJH publishes a list of all the hostels in Germany with descriptions of the facilities, photos, travel instructions, and rates. The website is: www.djh.de.

Lastly, for motorbikers, Germany is a member of the Motorbike Hotels International (tel. 097 768 18 00). These are hotels catering especially for motorbike travelers. Managers and many staff are active bikers themselves. First-time guests receive a "biker's pass," which makes every tenth night free of charge.

HEALTH AND SECURITY

Health and security concerns should be no greater in Germany than they are in the U.S.A. or the U.K. Medical facilities are among the most up-to-date in the world. Germany has both a national health service (government subsidized) and a private insurance system. You should review your insurance policy before you leave home to make sure it is valid internationally.

In order to see a doctor you will have to produce your insurance certificate. Routine appointments can be made with a local doctor, but specialist clinics and hospital emergency rooms or accident and emergency departments are available. If you need English-speaking support, the U.S. Embassy or the British Embassy should have details for the main cities.

Pharmacists have considerable freedom and expertise in recommending products to alleviate pain and other symptoms and will offer over-the-counter products. They also deal in natural or homeopathic products. Remember that the founder of homeopathy, Samuel Hahnemann, was a German. You may find that medications that require a prescription in the U.S.A. or U.K. can be bought over the counter in Germany.

Some German states have different telephone numbers for fire, police, and ambulance services. As a general rule try 110 for police and 112 for fire and ambulance, but if you are staying in an area for any length of time, check the local phone book for emergency numbers.

Violent crime is less common in Germany than in the United States and some parts of Britain. If you are a crime victim, report it to the police immediately. As anywhere, certain commonsense precautions are useful.

Useful Precautions
- Keep your car locked. There is a roaring trade in stolen cars.
- Don't leave baggage unattended in public places.
- Don't flash around expensive jewelry and camera equipment.
- Wear a zipped bag attached to your body to keep money, wallet, purse, and passport.
- Be aware of pickpockets. Cover your bag or purse in crowds such as carnivals or festivals.
- Make copies of your driver's license and passport and keep them apart from the originals.

chapter eight

BUSINESS BRIEFING

The conduct of business in Germany, as in Japan, involves a lot of diplomacy and protocol. How you do things is as important as what you do. Although more and more Germans are recognizing that "life is too short" for some of the niceties of traditional business

protocol, their foreign—mainly American and British—counterparts are constantly put at a disadvantage by their ignorance of particular aspects of German business practice.

Like Britain, Germany focuses on deals, data, and a moderately formal, reserved, and schedule-based business style. This is unlike the United States, which is less formal and more expressive in its business style.

> **Culturally Specific Business Drivers**
> - Office etiquette and protocol
> - Management styles
> - Leadership and decision making
> - Presentation and listening styles
> - Meetings and negotiation styles
> - Teamwork and managing disagreement
> - Hospitality and entertaining styles
> - Communication styles

We have already discussed hospitality and entertaining styles in Chapter 4, and we'll be looking at communication styles in Chapter 9.

OFFICE ETIQUETTE AND PROTOCOL

We have seen that German offices are much more formal than in English-speaking countries. People use surnames and really don't show much interest in each other's personal lives. On the other hand, visitors to German offices notice a highly informal style of dress, and the American and British "dress-down Friday" doesn't really apply. For meetings and dealing with visitors, however, formal wear is the norm. The exception is the bright red and green "Eurojacket" worn by some businessmen.

German business clothes are practical with a preference for well-cut, high-quality clothing.

The key is coordinated colors, styles, and patterns. "Business casual" in Germany may be taken to imply a casual attitude toward business. If in doubt, wear a dark suit or a sober jacket and tie. For women, conservative clothes are the best bet on first meeting; pantsuits are very acceptable.

Keep Your Jacket On!

A small point for men. If you are in a meeting or workshop with German managers, don't be the first to remove your jacket. German meetings tend to be quite formal, and removing a jacket is seen as a sign that work is over and that a more relaxed attitude can prevail!

If you go around a traditional German office you'll notice that it is mainly "closed door" and pretty quiet. People keep office doors shut for privacy and for meetings. If you need to interrupt, knock on the door and wait to be invited in. You may be used to looking for photos and mementoes in offices to provide clues about personal interests that can help in small talk and creating good relations. In most German offices, family photos and personal mementoes are not encouraged, and the "clear desk" policy means that no papers will be left out at the end of the day. As we have seen, it used to be perfectly possible for Germans to work for years alongside colleagues without ever using their first names or knowing much about their personal lives.

One thing that surprises foreign executives is the educational attainments of their German counterparts. A German CEO is quite likely to have a doctorate in his or her specialty, and in more conservative offices may expect to have it recognized. It is estimated that some 40 percent of the bosses of Germany's top one hundred corporations have

doctorates. A man would be addressed formally as Herr Doktor Schmidt and a woman as Frau Doktor Schmidt. In extreme cases, where a CEO has two doctorates, they would even be addressed as Herr or Frau Doktor Doktor Schmidt (one for each doctorate).

Once again, in old-fashioned firms it is important to address secretaries and support staff by their surnames. Waltraud Schmidt is "Frau Schmidt" not "Waltraud," or "Val," as it might be in the U.S.A. or the U.K. Some German executives, knowing American and British informality, will call you by your first name and invite you to use their first names, but in meetings be ready for the "code-switching" between German surnames and foreigner first names during the discussion. If you are speaking German in a German office, always use "*Sie*" until invited to do otherwise.

German office workers work from 8:00 a.m. till 5:00 p.m. Monday to Friday, and most conform to a thirty-seven-hour working week. To achieve this they may leave early on Friday, at around 3:00 p.m. Offices open early, from around 7:00 a.m., and close around 6:00 p.m. Many switchboards close early, at 4:00 p.m., although you can still contact people on their direct numbers beyond that time.

German holiday entitlement is a minimum of four weeks a year, rising for senior executives to up to six weeks. German workers often take their holiday in a block. If you add to this the twelve to fifteen legal holidays (depending on the state), and the generous sick and maternity and paternity leave, then you won't be surprised that some German executives are more accessible on voice-mail than personally. These absences can cause delays in reaching decisions or responding to queries, as delegation isn't common, due to the compartmentalization of German business.

The main holiday periods in German business are May, June, July, and August.

A characteristic of many German offices is that overtime is frowned upon. If you can't do your work in the time allotted, either you are personally disorganized or your job description is wrong. The admiration in some business cultures of overtime and "pulling an all-nighter to hit the deadline" is not shared by the Germans.

The Germans' attitude to office space is very different from that of the Americans or British, and is dominated by the need for greater personal space and the need for privacy. It is important, therefore, not to invade a German's office or personal space. Moving furniture around, for example, to get closer to a client, may be destabilizing for a German manager.

Appointments are made in advance and are adhered to strictly. Preferred times are 11:00 a.m. to 1:00 p.m. and 3:00 to 5:00 p.m. Avoid Friday afternoon as people often go home early. Punctuality is important, and you should shake hands on arriving and leaving with everyone involved in the meeting. Business cards are exchanged and will include academic titles as well as relevant business contact information. An accurate translation of your job title into German is necessary as it is important in Germany to match status with status.

When considering a relationship with a new partner, German companies very often begin with a small pilot deal. If this deal works, then it is the gateway to greater things. The worst thing a foreign contractor can do in seeking a relationship with a German company is to treat this small contract casually or to dismiss it as not worth their while.

The Germans believe in function more than relationships. Charming and agreeable business partners as they are, it is the wording of the contract and the fine print that matter most. Contract terms are considered "cast in concrete." This is not a problem for most American and British companies, but it may be for more relationship-oriented cultures where a degree of flexibility is appreciated.

MANAGEMENT STYLES

In German offices the management style is very direct. It is important to be the boss, to give and to receive orders clearly, and to carry them out to the letter. This, rather than imaginative interpretation, is the key to successful management and enables the Germans to coordinate complex projects and information successfully, albeit at the expense of flexibility. You'll notice that they get to the point quickly with very little small talk. Avoid being over-expressive. The Germans appreciate contained body language and not too much smiling, which they see as a false mannerism in a business environment. Above all, it is important not to make jokes in a business meeting. Before and after is fine, but business is serious and the facetiousness and irony of British jokes especially are felt to be totally out of place in this context, and will lead at least to the feeling that your behavior is inappropriate and at worst to a reputation as a "cowboy," and unreliable.

A characteristic of German management, in marked contrast to American and, to some extent, British practice, is the lack of praise. For Germans "excellence comes as standard" and you do not expect to be praised for doing your job. Praise for a German manager can seem patronizing, and staff appraisals, so important in American and British companies, are much less formal in the German environment, and may be carried out by supervisors rather than line managers and not at fixed times of the year. Reward for exceptional work may be a day off, to avoid extensive taxes payable on bonuses and other awards.

The key concerns for German managers are profit and the quality of the product or service.

As you might expect, the Germans are very insistent on deadlines, but the one thing that might justify a delay in delivery would be if the product quality were not felt to be satisfactory.

High-quality product and service, however, does not equate with "service with a smile." Although German service staff and product managers may be very personable and agreeable, it is axiomatic that efficiency and charm do not have to go together.

WOMEN IN MANAGEMENT

Women have equal rights under the German constitution and there is no discrimination on the basis of sex. There is legislation to protect the rights of workers who become pregnant and to encourage vocational and educational training.

However, although women constitute 50 percent of the workforce and have gained very high executive rank in both business and public life, 80 percent of executive positions are still held by men. To a lesser extent than in the U.S.A., but about equal with the U.K., the career "glass ceiling" still exists in Germany.

For foreign female executives working with German companies it is important to ensure that your status and responsibility within the company are never in doubt, and that the members of your team uphold this. Your business card should clearly state your company position and you should be able to demonstrate clearly and simply your areas of expertise and responsibility.

As far as women's dress goes, it is important to remember that the Germans are conservative dressers in business but very strong on clothes coordination. Do not dress sexily or wear ostentatious jewelry, especially at first. As you get to know the company better you may be able to adapt your clothes style as you wish.

German executives, particularly the older ones, will unconsciously adopt common courtesies toward women. These are simply courtesies, such as standing up for you on entrance, opening doors, walking on your left or nearest the curb, or lighting your cigarette (or, in exceptional situations among the older generation, kissing your hand on greeting). Such gallantry should be accepted graciously. Not to do so may cause embarrassment. If you do take exception to this behavior it is important to explain your position calmly and reasonably.

Women in business can easily avoid creating a sense of obligation by insisting on paying their own way. "Going Dutch" is quite acceptable and well understood in Germany society.

LEADERSHIP AND DECISION MAKING

Leadership in German companies is quite hierarchical. This is a legacy of Germany's relatively late industrial revolution, in the 1800s and early 1900s, when the social structure consisted of a very large number of workers supervised by a small number of managers. In addition, Germany still has many small and medium-sized family-owned businesses, with a strong controlling hand by the owner/founder and his or her family.

German companies are controlled by two separate boards, the *Aufsichtsrat* (supervisory board) and the *Vorstand* (board of management). The *Vorstand* is responsible for day-to-day operations, and the A*ufsichtsrat* is responsible for ratifying major budget and project descriptions.

Unlike American and British managers, who tended to have degrees in business or accounting, German managers used to be engineering specialists. Technical qualifications are still generally more highly respected in Germany than "soft" skills, and MBAs and business programs are a relatively recent phenomenon. Today's German managers are more likely to have degrees in the relevant discipline. The manager sets both the tasks and the standards for his or her team, and is expected to be a role model in his or her field.

A key feature of German management is the tight hierarchical reporting structure. German managers are much more "top-down" than their English-speaking equivalents. Many German managers in American and British multinational businesses have difficulty finding someone to report to and feel at a loss as a result.

In German companies the hierarchy is clear, and in reporting and seeking decisions you don't jump levels of management; if you do, you risk making an enemy of your manager and embarrassing the superior you have jumped the pecking-order to appeal to. In a contract negotiation it is important to respect the status of the manager who is your prime contact and not to enter into discussions with other managers unless you do it through him or her.

More than the Americans but less than the Japanese, German business people like to take time to reflect and consult on decisions. Since German companies are quite compartmentalized it is important to involve all the managers concerned and for them to discuss matters in some detail. The result is sometimes described as "analysis paralysis," as decisions are delayed to allow for this process to take place.

This means that the ability to make decisions rapidly is lacking in Germany. It also means that you must locate and deal with exactly the manager who has the precise responsibility and status to deal with your project or proposal. This, too, can take time and often causes frustration. A final problem can be that a decision, once made, is immutable. It can be hard for some German companies to introduce corrections once problems arise.

PRESENTATION AND LISTENING STYLES

The Germans respond well to thorough presentations, supported by detailed facts and specifications. They look for background information and history, and don't always respond to all-singing, all-dancing visuals. They like to feel that what they are buying into has been well received elsewhere, so it is important to include references and testimonials where you can. Some foreign presenters can be disconcerted by the pointedness and detail of the questions following a presentation.

A logical, clear presentation backed up by clear and extensive detail is important. Even if you only offer the broad conclusions, German audiences will expect you to have backup evidence and to be able to produce it on demand. They will also expect you to be able to give chapter and verse for any references quoted, business models used, and data presented. By the way, typing and spelling errors are as much a giveaway of a sloppy approach as scuffed shoes, so always double-check your documents.

One company representative, shaken by the barrage of questions and detailed interrogation and discussion that followed his presentation, said that he felt his presentation had been "torn to shreds." "On the contrary," said the German chairman, "If they hadn't liked your presentation they wouldn't have asked so many questions!"

MEETINGS AND NEGOTIATION STYLES

A fundamental feature of German industrial relations is the company Works Council (*Betriebsrat*). The Works Council has the right of consultation on every aspect of company policy that affects the workers in that company. This includes hiring and firing policy, working hours, holidays, pay, and job descriptions. They also have the right of consultation on company restructuring.

Therefore any German negotiator will have as a "background noise" the existence of and need to consult with the Works Council representative in any major decision.

Companies that have more than five nonmanagement employees must have a Works Council by law. Usually this is a voluntary post, but for companies with three hundred or more nonmanagement employees Works Council representation is a full-time job for at least one person. Government and public organizations also have Works Councils.

The Works Council makes it quite difficult for firms to lay off German workers. On the other hand, it creates a more integrated company. The German working environment tends to be more stable than in other countries, and company loyalty higher. It is certainly true that a German worker is more likely to stay in a job and to expand it, rather than to try to change jobs every two or three years to show a dynamic résumé, as is often the case in the U.S.A. or the U.K.

If disagreement within a German company deepens to the level of separation, it is difficult to fire people. If someone is to be dismissed, the procedures must be carefully followed, including consultation with the Works Council, which can appeal against the dismissal if they wish. Appeals are made to a special labor court, which, if it disagrees with the grounds for dismissal, can demand reinstatement or impose a fine for wrongful dismissal. If layoffs occur because of economic downturns, once again the Works Council must be consulted and guidelines followed regarding layoff benefit packages. If this sounds like an employee's charter, remember that there also exists a trial period on hiring that can last up to six months, in which either side can withdraw without problems.

Meetings and negotiations follow a formula well known to most business people. There will be an agenda (followed without deviation), action points, next steps, and time frames. What may be different is the personnel. Your German colleagues will be specialists in their fields and will 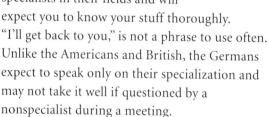 expect you to know your stuff thoroughly. "I'll get back to you," is not a phrase to use often. Unlike the Americans and British, the Germans expect to speak only on their specialization and may not take it well if questioned by a nonspecialist during a meeting.

Although top-level executives may attend the first meeting, or look in on a meeting, you should expect the detailed negotiations to take place with the middle management executives concerned.

However, top management will expect to approve the agreement, and this may take time.

The Germans, like the Japanese, prepare very thoroughly for their negotiations. They will think through their position and your position and prepare rebuttals for points they expect you to make. Once they have made their initial offer, they will stick to it in the face of pressure.

American and British negotiators often adopt a "high-low" range of bargaining tactics: start with a high entry point, and be prepared to exit at a fairly low point if they have to. They feel this is perfectly justified as they will go for a "what the market will bear" approach. The Germans prefer a much more realistic entry point and will bargain over a much smaller area. The rationale behind this is the German belief in "a fair price." They prefer to negotiate, with toughness, over a narrow range. It is important to be realistic in your expectations.

The best thing about German negotiators is that in all negotiations they are looking for common ground, and when they find it, it is the area where the deal will be finalized and also the basis for any compromise. An important corollary of this is that when a German says, "This is my last price," generally he or she means it. To push further may be to suggest that your German counterpart is cheating, and thus to lose the deal.

The use of lawyers also causes the Germans problems. In Germany oral agreements are considered firm, and most negotiations are conducted without lawyers until the point of drawing up the contract. The American habit of bringing lawyers in at the start of the negotiation can offend their German counterparts.

TEAMWORK AND MANAGING DISAGREEMENT

The German and American-British approaches to teamwork contain subtle but irritating differences, particularly at the level of team selection, problem solving, and decision making.

First of all, the Germans will choose their team members on the basis of specialization and seniority. The Americans and the British will take these into account, but give considerable importance to people who can get things done. These may be neither specialist nor senior, and this can be a recipe for friction if the relationship is not handled sensitively.

Another source of friction can be discussion styles. As we have seen, it is important for the Germans to understand the nature of the topic from which the solution will appear. The American-British tendency is to identify the problem and discuss the routes to solution. The length of the German ground-laying discussion can be frustrating for the English-speaking team members. Anything less, however, will be unsatisfying and not thorough enough for the German team members.

A third problem arises in the project planning and task delineation phase. Here again the Germans will want to go into detailed discussion in order to have a clear system and plan, and will exchange information in detail. The Americans and, to a lesser extent, the British will see this as part of the process of completing the task and will want to get straight down to business. The Germans dismiss this attitude as a "cowboy mentality," shooting first and asking questions later. As far as they are concerned the important ground-laying discussion process allows the group to reach a consensus on aims and means, and permits a far more rapid implementation.

The fourth problem arises when each team member gets down to work. This is when the Americans and the British expect lots of informal team and group meetings. The German members, however, expect to go off on their own, setting their own aims and researching and completing agreed-upon tasks. For the Americans and British, learning by doing is a cardinal principle. For the Germans, an agreed plan with the work divided up to fit the skills of team members is the most efficient way to proceed. Suddenly the English-speakers are deprived of day-to-day contact with their German colleagues, and this is made worse by the German adherence to company conventions regarding written technical rules, standards, company norms, project procedures, etc., which the German team members are expected to know and follow. The American and British outsiders may not even know of their existence, let alone be ready to apply them.

The Germans will tend to observe hierarchies and company structures within groups. American and British team members see these as restrictions "to be lifted for the duration." They will take the decisions reached at the project planning meetings as guidelines to be modified through discussion as the need arises. The Germans are likely to consider them binding.

Teamwork offers the English-speakers the opportunity to be more personal outside the formality of the "big" meeting. Both American and British teamworkers complain about the unwillingness of the Germans to discuss issues outside the formal work setting. The Germans misunderstand their wish to build up a rapport by talking about the task in detail and accuse them of asking unnecessary questions, the answers to which have already been agreed.

However, we are talking of tendencies toward different ways of working rather than black and white differences. Significantly, many of these rigid structures and attitudes are dying out fast, and many small to midsized international firms staffed by younger people have a more personal and relaxed atmosphere than you would find elsewhere. There is a new generation of Germans who are encouraged more openly by management, address each other informally, develop personal relationships in the workplace, and attend after-work events together, and who don't have to be as wary about certain issues as one might be under American management, which can be quite extreme.

German managers today are particularly sensitive to the needs of different nationalities in a multicultural team and of the necessity to accommodate them. The foreign team leader who takes these issues into account before the work starts, and who takes time to sort out problems as they arise, will ensure success. The team leader who doesn't, risks failure. This is particularly the case with mergers and acquisitions. In the 1990s about two thousand mergers and acquisitions took place in Germany with foreign buyers, the vast majority British or American firms. In the realm of small and medium-sized companies, over 50 percent of these mergers failed to take. Have we learned any lessons in the twenty-first century?

CONCLUSION

Germany is a highly attractive business partner, but only if you understand the German way of doing things. A trusted colleague, such as an agent or a German business partner, can be invaluable in mediating between the two sides in a negotiation, helping to smooth over potentially rough areas. Equally important is thorough preparation—not only for the presentation and the negotiation, but for the German ways of doing business.

chapter nine

COMMUNICATING

LANGUAGE

The quality of English-language education in Germany means that almost everyone you meet will speak English more than adequately, even if they answer "*ein Bisschen*" ("a bit") to the question, "Do you speak English?" But, perhaps because they don't feel foreigners make the effort, Germans will respond with more than usual warmth if you can just greet them in German and say "*Grüss Gott*," in Bavaria, or "*Guten Morgen*," "*Guten Tag*," or "*Guten Abend*" in the north.

German is spoken in Germany, Austria, in the German part of Switzerland, and in northern Italy, as well as in small enclaves around the world. It is no longer a world language, but in the nineteenth and early twentieth centuries it was the language of enlightenment, science, scholarship, and liberal values, and German researchers, thinkers, and philosophers led the world. Up to the 1990s it was the second language taught in Russian schools, and it appeared on menus and bilingual documents in Russia until its recent replacement by English.

If you see older books in German you will notice that they are often printed in a Gothic typeface, once common, but now almost totally abandoned in favor of the standard Roman script.

A branch of the Indo-European family of languages, German grew out of the languages spoken by the northern Asiatic tribes that migrated westward 2,000 years before Christ. It is related to the Scandinavian languages, Dutch, and English. Scholars have claimed to find German words in runic inscriptions on monuments, but the first recorded document in German is a Bible from the eighth century CE.

German children learn standard High German, or *Hochdeutsch*, the educated language of German-speaking peoples, but several regional dialects exist. Chief among these are the *Plattdeutsch* of Friesland and the Frisian islands in the north, and the *Switzerdeutsch* of the German-speaking cantons of Switzerland. The differences are of accent and vocabulary with some small grammatical changes, but the dialects are mutually comprehensible.

MAKING CONTACT

To communicate you have to make contact, and this is culturally defined, especially in business. Letters of introduction followed by telephone calls are considered the right way to do things. Cold-calling, out of the blue, is not usually welcomed. Not so long ago there used to be a convention that faxes or e-mails would be followed up with hard copy in the post, but many Germans have now abandoned this practice. However, it is always worth checking on your colleague's expectations. Job applications are normally typed, and a photograph is usually required.

TELEPHONES

The country code for Germany is 49 and there are area codes for each part of the country. The codes for the four main cities are:

Berlin	(0) 30
Hamburg	(0) 40
Frankfurt	(0) 69
Munich	(0) 89

Within the country dial 0 and the area code, and from overseas dial 49 and the area code without the 0. To dial out of Germany you usually dial 00 before the country code number.

For directory enquiries within Germany, dial 11833; for overseas directory enquiries, 11834. You can also use the phone book for residential numbers (*Fernsprechbuch*) or the Yellow Pages (*Gelbe Seiten*).

The telephone system in Germany is run by Telekom, which controls the network, and as in the U.S.A. and the U.K. there are alternative and possibly cheaper systems such as Arcor (dial 01070 before the number you want to reach), TelDelfax (01030), or Viatel (01079). You can choose a service by dialing the appropriate code before the number you are calling.

You'll notice that coin-operated public telephones are being phased out and are being replaced by phone cards. These you can buy at telephone shops and tobacconists. You'll also find vending machines at the main stations. International calls can be made through post offices. Go to the booth marked *Auslandsgespräche* (overseas calls). They can also be made with international calling cards or credit cards from public telephones. You will increasingly find Internet facilities available as well. Be careful about making calls from hotel bedrooms or restaurants.

The surcharges are very high and your phone bill could well exceed your room bill!

When the Germans answer the telephone they normally just state their surname. You, too, should identify yourself and the standard German form is "*Hier spricht Barry*" (literally, "Here speaks Barry," or "Barry speaking"). How do you ensure that people aren't already asleep when you call at night? By not calling after 10 p.m., unless of course you know your respondent's sleeping habits.

POST

"Snail mail" is still important in Germany. You'll see the yellow post boxes with the black post-horn symbol of the Deutsche Post all over Germany, and on mountain roads yellow vans will come hurtling past as they deliver parcels to mountain villages. Post offices open between 8:00 a.m. and 6:00 p.m., Mondays to Fridays, and between 8:00 a.m. and 12 noon on Saturdays. At stations and airports they may be open longer and even on Sundays. As you might expect, the German postal system is efficient, safe, and reliable, and next-day delivery is expected for letters posted at larger post offices before 9.00

a.m. There is usually one postal delivery a day. You can buy stamps either in the post office or from a machine outside (change is given in stamps), or at newsagents.

Post offices stock envelopes and parcel packaging. They also offer a range of other items and services to improve revenue. These include toys and collector's items related to the post office, gift services for sending flowers and presents, lottery tickets, and concert and theater tickets. You can pay utility charges, keep a post office checking account, transfer money, and carry out various other functions associated with banks. The post office can also arrange mail collection services for you. To find out more about the German postal service contact this website: www.deutschepost.de.

COMMUNICATION STYLES

The Germans value clear verbal communication and focus on the content rather than on the relationship. This is especially true in business. To the Americans and British, who are also content focused but place increasing emphasis on the relationship, this style of communication can seem overly serious. That said, there is much more common ground between young Germans and the youth of other countries brought up in an international pop culture.

Another factor influencing the Germans' communication style is education. Middle-class, educated Germans on the whole are taught to be clear, fact based, and also quite analytical. This means that they take matters seriously, and accept that if a subject is serious it can be complicated. While the whole thrust of American and British communication is toward directness and simplicity, German communication is often academically precise and involved. As a result, the Germans often complain that American and British comments are simplistic, whereas the English-speakers complain that the Germans are unnecessarily complicated.

The Germans strive for objectivity, and can do so ferociously. In the process their attempts to get at the truth and to examine issues in great detail can come across as demanding and even aggressive. As we saw in Chapter 8, presentations can be followed by alarmingly probing questioning if taken seriously. The focus on content and the effort to analyze its key features means that the discussion can get quite forceful. Once again, don't assume that people are getting angry; it is the tone of animated discussion. When the discussion is over the normal tenor of communication will resume. English-speakers are sometimes shocked by what they think has been an expression of personally directed anger. The lesson is, don't take it personally.

The same thing can happen in written communication, especially e-mails. The Germans will express themselves firmly and even strongly when disagreeing or rebutting an argument and then be surprised by the frigidity of response they receive from their British or American colleagues.

A British manager proposed to his German counterpart that a special discount be offered to a branch in Switzerland. He was surprised by the, to him, exaggerated response from Germany, not only telling him in no uncertain terms that this was not appropriate, but giving him an analysis of the relationship that made clear that this kind of decision was not within his competence or part of his responsibility. The British executive felt rudely and badly treated, and was quite frigid when he next met his German colleague. The German was his normal charming self, mildly concerned that his British colleague was having an "off day." A British or American executive would normally have been much more polite in telling his German counterpart to "butt out."

LOST IN TRANSLATION

German directness therefore directly affects the use of language. Whereas English-speakers commonly downgrade the directness of communication by using "would," "could," and "perhaps" (the British more than the Americans), the Germans, by contrast, will upgrade the directness of communication and use what seems to our ears quite strong language. They will use, even in English, words like "definitely" and "absolutely" more than we might.

At the same time, the Germans see no reason to "fudge" instructions. Foreign executive secretaries in German companies take time to get used to the directness of Germans who walk into their offices and say, "Give me that file, please," rather than, "Hi Carol, how's it going? Could I have the … file, please? Thanks a lot." For a German the social padding is a waste of time.

English-speakers tend to avoid "must" and "should" as they might cause offense. The Germans often don't realize this, and in translating directly into English from "*müssen*" and "*sollen*" they can quite unintentionally come across as overbearing. At the same time, the Germans don't shy away from a direct contradiction. "*Doch*," the German equivalent, of "Yes, but . . ." is often used to contradict flatly what has just been said. A native English-speaker would give credit to the previous thought by saying something like, "I see what you're saying, but . . ." before expressing disagreement and counterargument.

It is important to recognize when communicating with Germans that what we consider rude or inconsiderate may actually be perfectly acceptable in German discourse. If you are about to take offense at something said or written, ask before you get angry. If an e-mail or letter upsets you, get on the phone and question what was meant before you respond with anger or criticism. Remember that the Germans focus on the communication rather than on the person, whereas for the Americans and British the person is as important as the communication.

SERIOUSNESS AND HUMOR

German wit and repartee can be quick and very funny. However, the Germans do not feel it is necessary to tell jokes to get a message across. On the contrary, in business they can find it quite destabilizing. In school and at university German children learn to be as objective, serious, and impersonal as possible. This carries on into adult life. The German attitude is that if it is business, it needs to be taken seriously, and the American practice of using jokes as audience warm-ups, or the British use of humor to get over awkward moments in a meeting, can easily have the opposite effect on German decision makers.

Once again, attitudes can vary between older and younger members of the group, but be aware that the prevailing wind favors humor between meetings, not during them.

ANALYSIS AND DETAIL

The German way to solve a problem is first to analyze it in depth. The Anglo-American approach is more pragmatic: form a hypothesis and find a solution. Obviously analysis enters into both processes, but the Germans are taught to do it far more thoroughly and in greater detail. This is, once again, school training at work. The Germans have a word for it—*vertiefen*, going into depth. At bottom, this represents a belief that things are not simple; subjects need to be analyzed and pursued consistently until clarity is achieved. This entails speaking precisely, defining problems exactly, and being literal and scientific in approach. It also means sticking with the subject until you've got a result. This determined search for truth can get quite confrontational.

This analytical approach isn't just a business style. It's a life style. German friends will expect to talk about politics, philosophy, and attitudes to life and social issues. They will expect clarity. They will expect to reprove friends who they feel are not thinking things through, behaving inconsistently, or letting themselves down, and they will treasure directness and honesty rather than give each other an easy ride if they are wrong just because they are friends.

Germans are sometimes disappointed in American or British visitors with whom they find it difficult to have a really deep conversation. They find the constant moving from subject to subject superficial and careless. They find the urge to say things politely and not cause offense slippery. To their guests the Germans seem perfectionist, elitist, and determinedly, to use an expression coined by a German-speaking psychologist and philosopher, "anal." There is a recipe here for cross-cultural misunderstanding, unless, of course, you understand where your colleague is coming from.

HONOR
And here's another cross-cultural problem. One of the reasons German children are taught to watch their language is that what they say represents their honor. The Germans set great store by doing what they say they will do according to the recognized rules and nothing more. The idea of exaggerating your qualifications or citing your successes in order to boost your profile to get a better job is unacceptable by German standards of honor and objectivity. "Keeping your options open" is not necessarily the honorable option for a German. This is a country where oral agreements are morally binding. A German's word quite literally is his, or her, bond.

Honorable behavior entails keeping your commitments. This is important in business communications. It is vital for foreign negotiators to be very clear about what has been agreed and what has not. It is not uncommon for deals to fail because what the Americans or British considered to be "thinking aloud" was taken by their German counterparts to be a commitment. The Germans can be unforgiving about what they see to be unreliability or lack of credibility. An example of the social confusion that can be caused is the American and British use of phrases such as "I'll call you" or "We must have lunch" as expressions of goodwill. The Germans see them as a commitment, and are upset if they are not followed up.

Part of an honorable way of expressing yourself is to be as clear and as unambiguous as possible. One way of doing this is to strive for impersonal objectivity in your speech. There is even a term for this, *Sachlichkeit*, objectivity. You attain objectivity by the use of the pronoun "one" (*man kann*, one can), by the use of the passive voice, and, above all, by saying what you mean and meaning what you say. The Germans are wary of people who respond personally if their opinions are attacked, and they consider the idea of not upsetting the applecart, and "keeping things friendly," as suspect. They also find the American "confessional" style of revealing personal information in the search for common ground astonishing and sometimes demeaning.

CONVERSATION

Lest you think that to be German is to be prosaic, boring, and preoccupied with minutiae, let us finish this discussion with a mention of *Gemütlichkeit*—a cosy or jolly atmosphere. The Germans in the right place at the right time, almost always out of the office, enjoy relaxed, leisurely conversation over a drink or food, which they describe as *Unterhaltung*, or simple conversation. This is much lighter than the analytical approach to discussion presented earlier. Taking place at home, in a *Bierstube*, or a restaurant, the conversation is light, and full of humor and companionship—another facet of the "serious" Germans.

BODY LANGUAGE

Some social scientists claim that up to 80 percent of communication is nonverbal. They probably haven't studied the Germans, who tend to be reserved and introverted, and who try not to draw attention to themselves. Facial expressions tend to be less demonstrative than those of the Americans and British, and smiles to be kept for family and close friends, although the Germans enjoy the smiling aspect of U.S. life. Posture tends to be straight. German children are still taught to sit up straight, and "laid back" postures, although adopted by the young, are not well regarded.

Some German Gestures

- The German equivalent to crossing fingers to wish for luck is to press your thumbs. If a German says, "I'll press my thumbs for you," it means "Good luck." This may be accompanied by a fist with the thumb inside.
- Like the British, Germans tap the side of their head with their index finger to indicate "You're crazy!"
- A mistake that can cost you money is if you raise your index finger in a bar to order a beer – you may get two. Germans start counting with their thumbs, not their index finger.
- Most surprising, if you finish a presentation at a meeting, instead of applause you may be met with a rumbling noise as your German audience rap the table with their knuckles in appreciation.
- Children sometimes stick their thumbs between the first and second fingers of a fist to make a face. Stop them doing it in Germany: it's an obscene gesture.

The old joke that in Germany you shake hands with everything that moves, whenever it moves really means that you should shake hands with everyone present, both on meeting them and on leaving them.

Body language, then, in Germany is less expressive than in parts of the U.S.A., but similar to Britain, and visitors and negotiators should consider moderating their body language to what they observe around them. That being said, like every country, Germany has its peculiarities.

CONCLUSION

An experienced observer of European culture once said, "If you see something that surprises you, angers you, or that you find completely ridiculous, you may be in the presence of a cultural characteristic." He also said that the people who display the greatest cultural differences may be the ones who look most like you. For the majority of Caucasian Americans, Britons, and northern Europeans, the Germans do "look like us," and we should be careful not to assume that just because they "talk the talk," they necessarily "walk the walk." If you are upset by something said or done, take a breath and do not react immediately. If you were to ask people why they have behaved or said things in a particular way, nine times out of ten the explanation would be completely innocuous. A lot of cultural-awareness building consists of not allowing unfamiliar attitudes to throw you. Observing, hearing, feeling, and then talking, is the way to build and enjoy good relations with the people of this culturally rich and dynamic country.

Appendix: Simple Vocabulary

Signs

Abfahrt
departure

Aukunft
arrival

Ausgang
exit [on foot]

Ausfahrt
exit [for vehicles]

Besetzt
Engaged

Damen/D
Ladies

Drücken
push

Eingang
entrance [on foot]

Einfahrt
entrance [for vehicles]

Frei
Free, vacant

Gefahr
danger

Geschlossen
closed

Herren/H
gentlemen

Kein
no (Kein Eingang, no entry)

Notausgang
emergency exit

Offen
open

Polizei
police

Rauchen verboten
no smoking

Umleitung
diversion

Verboten
prohibited

Toiletten
toilets

Ziehen
pull

Zoll
customs

Phrases

Auf Wiedersehen
Good bye

Bitte, Bitte schön
Please (also used for "Don't mention
it/it's a pleasure," and "Can I help you?")

**Danke, Danke sehr, Danke schön,
Vielen Dank**
Thank you

Entschuldigen Sie, Verzeihung
I am sorry/Excuse me

Guten Abend
Good evening

Guten Aufenthalt!
Have a nice stay!

Guten Morgen
Good morning

Gute Nacht
Good night

Guten Tag
Good day
(greeting used throughout the day)

Haben Sie Zimmer frei?
Do you have any rooms free?

Ich verstehe (das) nicht
I don't understand

Ist hier frei?
Is this seat free?

Ja
Yes

Nein
No

Sprechen Sie Englisch?
Do you speak English?

Viel Spaß!/Viel Vergnügen!
Have fun!/Enjoy yourself!

Vorsicht!/Achtung!
Look out!

Wann...?
When...?

Wie bitte?
I beg your pardon?

Wieviel kostet...?
How much is...?

Wo ist...?
Where is...?

Wo kann ich telefonieren?
Where is a phone I can use?

Further Reading

There is a wide range of books on different aspects of Germany.
Here are a few titles to start with.

Craig, Gordon A. *The Germans.*
London: Penguin, 1991.

Dawes, Nick. *Living and Working in Germany.*
London: Survival Books, 2000.

Fulbrook, Mary. *A Concise History of Germany.*
Cambridge: CUP, 1991.

Jones, Alun. *The New Germany: A Human Geography.*
Chichester: John Wiley & Sons, 1994.

Lord, Richard. *Culture Shock! Germany: A Guide to Customs and Etiquette.*
Portland, Oregon: Graphic Arts Center Publishing, 1996/London:
Kuperard, 2002.

Lord, Richard. *Succeed in Business: Germany.*
London: Kuperard, 1998.

McLachlan, Gordon. *The Rough Guide to Germany.*
London: Rough Guides, 2001.

Nees, Greg. *Germany.*
Yarmouth, Maine: Intercultural Press, 2000.

Phillips, Jennifer. *In the Know in Germany.*
New York: Living Language, 2001.

Schulte-Peevers, Andrea, et al. *Lonely Planet: Germany.*
Melbourne/Oakland/London,/Paris: Lonely Planet Publications, 2002.

Stern, A. Z. and Joseph A. Reif (eds.). *Everyday German.*
London: Kuperard, 1991.

German. A Complete Course. New York: Living Language, 2002.

German Business Companion. The Language Guide for Business.
New York: Living Language, 1998.

Index